S0-CPF-438

PASSPORT To New York Restaurants 1992

by
John F. Mariani
&
Peter D. Meltzer

Published by
Passport Press, Ltd.
P.O. Box 1003
New York, N.Y. 10021
Tel (212) 772-3942
Fax (212) 535-8174

Cover by David Blumenthal, Creative Combinations
Maps by David Lindroth, Inc.
Typography By Fine Composition, Inc.
Printed by Montrose Publishing Co.

© Passport Press

(ISBN 0-937413-06-2)

ABOUT THE AUTHORS

All reviews were compiled by food and wine critics John F. Mariani and Peter D. Meltzer.

John Mariani has authored four books on American dining. The first, *The Dictionary of American Food and Drink* (Ticknor & Fields, 1983) was hailed as the "American Larousse Gastronomic." He followed Dictionary with a specialized guide, *Eating Out: Fearless Dining in Ethnic Restaurants* (Quill, 1985), and edited *Mariani's Coast-to-Coast Dining Guide.* (Times Books 1986). His latest book, *America Eats Out*, an illustrated history, was published by William Morrow in the fall of 1991.

Currently, Mariani is Food & Travel Correspondent for *Esquire*. He writes a regular column on New York restaurants for *Food & Wine* and contributes to *Harper's Bazaar*. Further, he is restaurant expert for the Prodigy Service. John Mariani co-hosted the Public Broadcast television program "Crazy for Food."

Peter Meltzer is publisher and Editor-in-Chief of the *PASSPORT* guides. He has been tracking the restaurant scene since he began *The Wine Spectator*'s "Grand Award Profiles," an annual feature highlighting the best restaurant wine lists in America, which he authored from 1981-1990.

Meltzer is presently Editor-at-Large for *FOOD ARTS* magazine and he also contributes to *Town & Country*. In addition, Meltzer has co-hosted and co-directed the television and video pilots, "The Wine Magazine" and "Les Grands Chefs."

CONTENTS

INTRODUCTION

Last year was indeed a watershed for many New York restaurants. Between the Gulf War and the recession, there was a noticeable decline in expense-account dining, and a shift to more casual eating habits. Some restaurateurs reported volume was off by as much as 40 percent. In fact, we lost over 40 restaurant listings from last year's PASSPORT; noteworthy passings like Laurent, Prunelle, La Tulipe, Aurora, Le Cygne, Toscana, and Huberts; old favorites like Chez Louis, Dieci, Rusty's, and Le Zinc; even a couple of trendy newcomers like 150 Wooster and Punsch.

Yet on the positive side, we actually gained an equal number of new entries, despite the economy. Foremost is JoJo, a French bistro owned by Jean-Georges Vongerichten, previously chef at Restaurant Lafayette. Gray Kunz, formerly of Adrienne, now presides over Lespinasse in the newly restored St. Regis Hotel. And speaking of hotels, The Sherry Netherland is once again home to Harry Cipriani, after a four year hiatus. Marilyn Frobuccino, formerly of Arizona 206, now offers an eclectic menu at Mimosa. Le Bernardin's Dominic Cerrone is now chef at Solera, NYC's newest Spanish restaurant. Midtown, Al Bustan serves up Middle Eastern fare on the site that once housed Le Bistro.

The list of openings post-publication is smaller than usual, and largely confined to local eateries. Nonetheless, there are several to watch for: The successful team of Vince Orgera and Eddie Schoenfeld (Vince & Eddie's, q.v.) will open both Fishin' Eddie (73 West 71st Street, 874-3474) and Chop Suey Looey's Litchi Lounge (1345 Avenue of the Americas, 262-2020). Christian Delouvrier, formerly of The Parker Meridien, will debut at Les Célébrités (160 Central Park South in the Hotel Nikko, 247-0300). Planet Hollywood, more of a stage set than a stellar eatery, will no doubt create a big splash (140 West 57th Street 333-7827).

Events of the past year send mixed signals from the restaurant community. While it is no longer inconceivable to get a table on short notice at restaurants where it once took weeks, there are still waiting lists at many popular places. On the other hand, prices in many expensive restaurants have dropped, and some are now offering special fixed price menus at bargains unthinkable a year or two ago. Another undeniable consequence of the turmoil has been a wide range of charming "downscale" neighborhood restaurants where main courses run well under $20.

One aspect of New York's dining experience hasn't changed a bit. The city still remains the nation's gastronomic epicenter—offering a great deal of everything—from the finest French food to the best bargain bistro, the most sophisticated Italian dining to the trendiest trattoria. Whether you are in search of authentic Southwestern fare, Thai dishes or Japanese sushi, you are sure to find it in PASSPORT TO NEW YORK RESTAURANTS 1992.

HOW TO FIND A RESTAURANT

The restaurants in PASSPORT are laid out geographically by neighborhood, from Lower Manhattan through the Bronx and beyond. Headers at the top of each page indicate general location. Brand new this year are 11 pages of maps, which precisely pinpoint a restaurant's position. So no matter what part of New York you are in, PASSPORT provides an appropriate restaurant.

Although New York's grid pattern makes navigation relatively easy, a few street terms warrant definition: Lower Manhattan—for our purposes, from the southernmost tip of Manhattan Island to Fulton Street. Chinatown—traditionally bounded by Canal, Worth, Baxter and Bowery. The spine of Little Italy is Mulberry Street, bounded by Grand Street. TriBeCa—The Triangle Below Canal Street. SoHo—the area South of Houston Street in the vicinity of West Broadway. Greenwich Village—bounded by

Houston Street on the south, 14th Street on the north. The East Village extends from Fifth Avenue to Avenues A, B, and C; The West Village from Fifth Avenue to West Street.

You can always search PASSPORT by location. Otherwise check our alphabetical listing. (It also gives our star ratings, but for a comparative overview, see our star index.) If, instead, you want to choose a restaurant by cuisine, consult our Food Index. Other helpful indexes include Good Value, Sunday Suggestions, For Children, Open Late, Worthy Wine Lists, and Take-out. "Where to Find the Best," a selection of what we think are some of the best dishes in town and where to find them, and "Where Should I Go For," suggestions for special occasion dining, are also listed in back. Don't overlook our ethnic dining dictionary or our vintage wine chart.

RATINGS & SYMBOLS

Food		Wine List
★★★★★	Extraordinary	🍷🍷🍷🍷
★★★★	Excellent	🍷🍷🍷
★★★	Very Good	🍷🍷
★★	Good	🍷
★	Fair	🍷
●	Poor	

$$$$$	$50 and up	$$	$20
$$$$	$40	$	$10
$$$	$30	1/2	$ 5

↻ A NYC institution or special place—although not necessarily for the food.

Our dollar signs refer to the cost of a dinner without wine or liquor, before tax and tip. Since the price of a bottle of wine can vary from $15 to well over $150, with an additional 25% to cover tip and tax, it is impossible to predict the full cost of a meal. Dinner for two can run from as little as $30 at a modest restaurant to upwards of $200 at a fancy one. Expect to pay about $75–$100 a couple on the average.

MORE ON PRICES

It's worth noting that prices for lunch tend to be much lower than dinner at stellar spots, so that you can dine regally at the most deluxe restaurants for as little as $30 per person at lunch, whereas that same meal might cost you $60 at dinner. Many haute cuisine restaurants offer three-course, fixed price dinner menus, which are usually a bit less than ordering à la carte. But be warned about supplements and surcharges on such menus. If the waiter mentions a special, don't hesitate to ask how much it costs.

RESERVATIONS

Even though the past season has witnessed a decline in restaurant business, that doesn't mean you can show up at any hour and expect to be seated immediately. Reservations are always a good idea and, more often than not, essential at our top-rated restaurants. Weekdays are easier than weekends and lunch easier still. You'd also be surprised how many times no-shows open up a table even on a Saturday night, so it's worth a last-minute call to find out. Another ploy to snare an otherwise booked table is to make a very early (say, 6:00 PM) or quite late (9:30 PM) reservation. Even the best restaurants often have tables at those hours. Sometimes you may be asked for a confirmation telephone number. Always phone when you intend to cancel.

HOURS OF BUSINESS

Many of the restaurants reviewed in PASSPORT serve lunch and dinner seven days a week. A survey of all the establishments listed here showed that over 250 were open on Sunday alone. (See our index for recommendations.) But since days and even hours of business are subject to change, be sure to check before you arrive on the restaurant's doorstep.

New York restaurants are generally open for lunch from noon until 2:30 or 3:00 PM. Dinner reservations are normally accepted from 6:00 PM (expect pre-theater and early evening dining to be rushed; there's another seating on the way) until 10:00 or 10:30 PM, so that movie and theater-goers can be accommodated in most places. Call first to avoid finding yourself at the lone table while the staff sweeps up. (Consult our index of restaurants open until midnight and beyond.)

DRESS

NYC restaurants tend to be fairly formal, so that a suit, or jacket and tie are often required, usually recommended, and always in good taste, especially in midtown and the Upper East Side. In the Village, SoHo and TriBeCa, and many ethnic restaurants, dress tends to be more casual. It's a good idea to call and find out beforehand.

SMOKING, SEATING & SIBERIA

New York City law now stipulates that restaurants with more than 50 seats set aside a non-smoking section. Make your preference known when you reserve. Many people worry about another aspect of the "seating game" in deluxe or trendy restaurants, namely, who gets the best tables and how to avoid getting placed in "Siberia." The best tables are customarily doled out to regular customers or celebrities, while newcomers may be seated elsewhere. It should not be assumed, therefore, that not getting a "A" table is a deliberate slight.

If you do get a table you find truly awful—next to the restroom, the kitchen, or service station—politely request another. If available, the maître d' should move you elsewhere; perhaps not the window table, but a good one. Whatever you do, do NOT "grease the palm" of the maître d' on the spot. If you have gotten good service and liked where the maître d' seated you, you may choose to give him a tip (anywhere from a few dollars to $10 or more if you wish to be remembered) on the way out, but it is in no way mandatory.

TIPPING

Standard tip is 15%, or 20% of the bill, pre-tax. Double the NYC sales tax, and you'll get the figure for a 16.5% tip. You don't need to tip the maître d' (see above) except for special service endered. Most service staffs pool their tips at the end of each evening (busboys and bartenders are given a share), so it is not necessary to separate your tip in cash or on your credit card. If you do want to separate your tip in a deluxe restaurant, give 15% to the waiter and 5% to the captain.

Otherwise, just leave between 15% and 20% in one lump sum. Wine stewards are tipped only if they perform a special service, like decanting a rare wine or advising you throughout a multi-course meal. Then a tip of a few dollars (more still if you have uncorked a series of stellar vintages) is in order. Coatcheck attendants usually get a dollar per coat. At the bar, a tip of a dollar on a $5-$10 drink order is just fine.

CREDIT CARDS

Unless otherwise indicated, the restaurants listed in PASSPORT accept all major credit cards.

CUSTOMIZED PASSPORTS

What better premium for your company than a customized, pocket-sized guide to New York restaurants? For professional advice on business lunches or a special night on the town, PASSPORT is a gift item that sets itself apart from all others. Quell corporate entertaining worries with PASSPORT. See order form located in the center of the book for information about customized books, or telephone (212) 772-3942, fax (212) 535-8174.

INDEX

x

LOWER MANHATTAN

☼★★ **FRAUNCES TAVERN**—54 Pearl Street (corner of Broad and Pearl)—269-0144—An evocative American restaurant within an historic re-structure (where Washington bade farewell to his troops in 1783), Fraunces Tavern is one of the last bits of Colonial New York remaining, and the Museum upstairs is a delight. Downstairs there's a barroom and dining room that fill up with the bulls and bears of Wall Street, who come for everything from a hearty breakfast of oatmeal and eggs to lunch and dinners that focus on American classic dishes like steaks, chops, and seafood. $$$$ ♥♥

★★ **AMERICAN HARVEST**—3 World Trade Center (in the Vista International Hotel)—938-9100—The folk art motif and genteel atmosphere make this a wonderful oasis amid the steel and granite of the area. The restaurant serves fine traditional regional American cooking—Maine lobster, Michigan baby white asparagus—and there's an eclectic Sunday brunch in the more casual Greenhouse restaurant next door. $$$ ♥♥♥

☼★★ **WINDOWS ON THE WORLD**—1 World Trade Center—938-1111—Perched on the 107th floor of the World Trade Center with a spectacular view of the city unfolding beneath, this is one of the country's most awesome restaurants. During the day Windows is a private business club, but at night it's all open to the public. The simpler food items such as paillard of chicken or veal, good rack of lamb and fine American chocolate cakes are often the best choices. The wine list at Windows is one of the most extensive in the country, with tremendous breadth and depth of choice and very fair prices. In fact, Windows is so committed to wine that it actually offers a special dining experience for the oenophile at ★★★ **CELLAR IN THE SKY**—a compact, enclosed dining room within the restaurant proper—where a seven course menu with wine is served with five carefully matched wines at a fixed price of $90.00. ($$$$ at Windows.) Reserve well in advance and consult the long-range

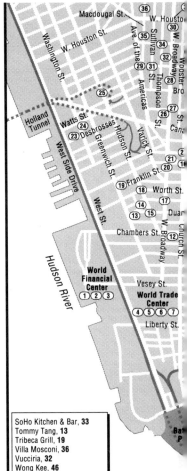

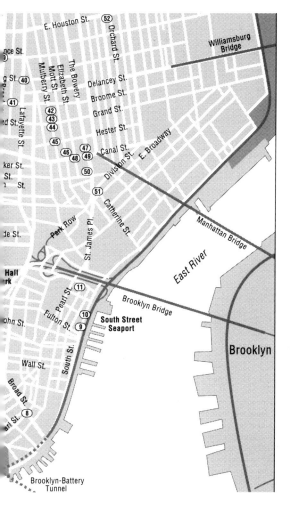

E. Houston St.

Orchard St. (52)

Williamsburg Bridge

nce St. 9

g St. (40)

The Bowery
Elizabeth St.
Mott St.
Mulberry St.

Delancey St.

Broome St.

Grand St.

(41)

d St. (42)
(43)
(44)

Lafayette St.

Hester St.

(45)

(46) (47)
(48) (49)

Canal St.

E. Broadway

ker St.
St.
St.

(50)

Division St.

(51)

Catherine St.

Manhattan Bridge

de St.

Park Row

St. James Pl.

East River

Hall
rk

Pearl St. (11)

Brooklyn Bridge

ohn St.

Fulton St. (10)
(9)

South Street
Seaport

Wall St.

South St.

Brooklyn

Broad St.

rl St. (8)

Brooklyn-Battery
Tunnel

3

weather forecast beforehand. ♛♛♛♛♛

★★★ **THE MARKET DINING ROOMS**—5 World Trade Center—938-1155—For steaks, chops, and seafood, this is the best in Lower Manhattan. Very masculine atmosphere, excellent wine list. Located on the concourse of the World Trade Center and it's very noisy. Closed Sunday. $$$$ ♟♟♟

★★ **HUDSON RIVER CLUB**—4 World Financial Center—786-1500—The World Financial Center houses some splendid restaurants. One of the most attractive is the Hudson River Club, which looks out over the mouth of the Hudson River. This is real corporate dining style—golden paneling, lots of brass, thick carpeting—and the ambiance is civil, if not exciting. The menu, under chef Waldy Malouf, features the products and ingredients of the Hudson River Valley in season, and while the food is quite good, it's unfortunately not very special. $$$$ ♟♟♟

★★★ **LE PACTOLE**—2 World Financial Center—945-9444—Romeo Gobbi, former maître d' at Le Cirque, oversees this large, formal dining room with a grand panorama of the river, and it's the best restaurant of the dozen or so in the World Financial Center. The food is what they call "retro cuisine," which is an attempt to bring back classic dishes that had become clichés but which now taste new again. The menu is very large, yet the kitchen does most things very well. There's even a good cheese tray. Magret of duck and confit with roasted potatoes, brandade with caviar, roasted chicken with bacon and scallion vinaigrette, gratin de fruits. Le Pactole has excellent banquet facilities. $$$$½ ♟♟♟

★★ **AU MANDARIN**—200/250 Vesey Street (in the World Financial Center)—385-0310—A very safe Chinese restaurant catering to a business clientele, situated on the ground floor of The American Express Tower. Au Mandarin boasts an inviting, contemporary look. Crispy spring roll, steamed Shanghai dumplings, General Tso's chicken, and beef tangerine are all adequately prepared if a tad unexciting. Fixed price $30 at dinner or a la carte. $$$ ♟♟

♡★ **SOUTH STREET SEAPORT**—This is not a

restaurant but an historic district impeccably restored to its 19th-C. maritime grandeur, and it is very pleasant to explore. Lunch or dinner at one of the many restaurants here is also something of an adventure. You can expect to find a host of rather average fast food boutiques serving every imaginable type of ethnic cooking. Best bet is ★ **SLOPPY LOUIE'S**—92 South Street—509-9694—a very old place specializing in seafood and antique charm, though a bit touristy. $$$ 🍷🍷

★★½ **BRIDGE CAFE**—279 Water Street (off Dover Street)—227-3344—This very old, extremely amiable little café is in the South Street Seaport area—but ask for specific instructions how to find it before venturing out. The place evokes a simpler era in New York, and it's always warm and happy. The menu is small but changes often, and the food is basic and wholesome. Pastas not the strong point. Good breads, fried calamari, duck with wild rice, fruit crumble. $$$ 🍷

CHINATOWN, LITTLE ITALY, TRIBECA AND SOHO

★½ **ECCO**—124 Chambers Street (near West Broadway)—227-7074—There's a certain raffish, neighborhood feel about this place, and in fairness, the antipasti are terrific. But the casual diner does not receive the kind of attention he deserves. There's even a $6 "extra plate charge." Under the circumstances, why not head uptown to Campagnola (a sibling) for the same menu in more pleasant surroundings? $$$ 🍷🍷

★★★ **TOMMY TANG**—323 Greenwich Street (near Reade Street)—334-9190—Still going very strong, this Hollywood transplant to TriBeCa attracts homebound Wall-Streeters and a mixed bag of area residents and fans of Thai cuisine from all over. The high-ceilinged, geometric design creates a lively backdrop for some serious eating. It's a good bet to share a variety of appetizers. Start with chicken saté, "naked" shrimp, or spicy chicken and pork wontons.

For a main course, try the ginger beef with black beans, the blackened whole chili fish, grilled prawns with panang curry or Siam chicken. Home-made sorbets serve as a refreshing finale. $$$ 🍷

★★★★ **BOULEY**—165 Duane Street (near Hudson Street)—608-3852—An artfully restored TriBeCa structure that boasts dramatic arched ceilings, sedate lighting, impressionistic landscapes, and handsome furniture. Owner David Bouley is a sensible chef; his food is exciting without being trendy—sea scallops with sea urchins, braised salmon in bandol wine, yellowfin tuna, frogs' legs served in a watercress consommé of Canadian chanterelles, venison with root vegetables and leek gratin, hot Valrhona chocolate soufflé with chocolate sauce. Bouley's popularity has soared over the past few years. Regrettably, the price of prominence can mean up to a 45 minute wait in a crowded anteroom for a confirmed table, plus frustrating delays between courses. Reserve early—at 6 or 6:30 PM—to be sure of a table. Fixed price five-course menu is $65. A la carte $$$$$ 🍷🍷🍷

★★½ **DUANE PARK CAFE**—157 Duane Street (near Hudson Street)—732-5555—A simple and soothing addition to the TriBeCa scene. It's small, comfortable, and sincere, and the food quite satisfying, but this is not a destination restaurant. House cured basil gravlax, goat cheese in phyllo, rigatoni with a duck confit, pan fried Cajun ribeye, crispy skate with ponzu. $$$½ 🍷

★★ **THE ODEON**—145 West Broadway (at Thomas Street)—233-0507—Housed in an Art Deco 1930s cafeteria, this was the first notable restaurant in the TriBeCa neighborhood and the first to be adopted by the SoHo art set, who still makes it a major stamping ground after midnight. At times it seems as if everybody here wears black, looks slightly world weary, and appears to know each other. The bistro fare is no longer of the same high quality, but The Odeon remains a great spot to plug into the "scene" in this artsy district. Grilled chicken, steak frites. $$$½ 🍷🍷🍷

★★★½ **CHANTERELLE**—2 Harrison Street (near

Hudson)—966-6960—An exceedingly stark setting—bare yellow walls dominated by massive floral arrangements—is the back-drop for chef-owner David Waltuck's intricate and impeccably executed fare. His menus are limited, but change frequently. Chanterelle continues to draw a loyal following, although its prices seem out of sync with establishments of similar standing. Crazy salad, dumplings with lobster and shrimp, oxtail terrine, grilled salmon with smoked salmon cream, grilled halibut, loin of lamb with savory and saffron, millefeuille of pineapple and rum. For a whopping $15 supplement, you can order a cheese course. Extensive but expensive wine list. Now serving lunch. Fixed price, three-course dinner menu $68. Six-course menu $87. 🍷🍷🍷

★★★½ **TRIBECA GRILL**—375 Greenwich Street (near Franklin Street)—941-3900—With Robert DeNiro, Mikhail Baryshnikov, Christopher Walken, and other celebs as partners, TriBeCa Grill wouldn't need to serve more than burgers and chili to be a hit, but partner Drew Nieporent, owner of the renowned Montrachet nearby, has made sure the kitchen, under chef Don Pintabona, is first rate and that all customers are treated equally, even on the craziest nights. The large brick dining room, with its grand bar salvaged from Maxwell's Plum, has well-spaced tables and real vitality, as do dishes like lobster gazpacho, cavatelli with pecorino, lobster raviolo with grilled scallops, pan-seared duck with white bean ragout, potato pancakes "Vonnas," and lemon crème brûlée with poppyseed crust. $$$½ 🍷🍷

★★ **EL TEDDY'S**—219 West Broadway (between Franklin and White Streets)—941-7070—Lots of glitter and tile—the legacy of restaurants past—make this one of the city's more offbeat interiors. It's also one of the few spots where margaritas are made to measure with your choice of several different Tequilas. Masa tarts with chicken and chile Pequin, cactus salad with jicama, portobello mushroom with salsa verde, shrimp marinated in lime and tequila, charred tuna steak with salsa fresca. Amex only. $$½ 🍷

★★★★★ **MONTRACHET**—239 West Broadway (near

White Street)—219-2777—Set in a quaint TriBeCa location and presided over by the dedicated Drew Nieporent, Montrachet remains one of the most consistently satisfying restaurants in NYC, despite the fact that Nieporent now divides his time between this location and his latest sensation, TriBeCa Grill on nearby Greenwich Street. Chef Deborah Ponzek is equally serious about the essential flavors of her ingredients, and care is shown in the preparation of every dish. The wines are especially well-chosen and include unique French country selections directly imported by sommelier Daniel Johnnes, along with priceless Burgundies. Montrachet is priced somewhat below comparable establishments, and the atmosphere is also more casual than one might expect. Sautéed foie gras, peasant soup, red snapper with red peppers and lemon, guinea hen with mushroom sauce and squash purée, salmon with lentils, pheasant with olives, apricot tart. There are fixed price menus at $25, $32, $45, as well as à la carte offerings. Lunch on Friday only. Amex only. $$$$ 💬💬💬💬

★★★ **ARQUA**—281 Church Street (near White Street)—334-1888—This chic trattoria looks and sounds very Italian—bare peach walls, and, depending on the hour you dine, a deafening noise level. Nonetheless, Arqua draws a sophisticated TriBeCa crowd as the place begins to fill up after 8:30 PM. The food is very satisfying and unpretentious. Cotechino sausage and lentils, cannelloni, mattonella d'Arqua, pear tart. Amex only. $$$½ 💬💬

★★ **BAROCCO**—301 Church Street (near Walker Street)—431-1445—Instant popularity brought problems with overbooking to this attractive downtown trattoria—but delays have lessened as the novelty factor died down. Generally good risottos, fettucine with artichokes, grilled swordfish, veal chop. Open Sunday. Dinner only. $$$½ 💬💬

★★½ **PONTE'S**—39 DesBrosses Street (off the West Side Drive)—226-4621—For a quarter century now Ponte's has been a favorite of Wall Streeters, Bridge-and-Tunnel commuters, and lovers of solidly old-fashioned, if uninspired, Italian American food served in an atmosphere of unbridled la dolce vita. Through the extravagantly decorated dining room, captains wheel a blackboard menu to your table, describe the specials, bring you endless quantities of bread and then serve you portions of food that would daunt Pavarotti. The gnocchi with fresh tomato, the lobster arrabbiata and the veal chop are all of a very high quality. The singing guitar player is not. Ponte's is a throwback in the best sense and a place you couldn't fail to enjoy. $$$½ ♙♙

★★★ **CAPSOUTO FRERES**—451 Washington Street (near Canal Street)—966-4900—Its setting in a glorious old landmark building, its view of the Hudson, and its own soaring architectural design make this a stand-out restaurant in TriBeCa. The brothers Capsouto were among the first to offer Mediterranean and Provencal cuisine, and they do it very well indeed. The soft shell crabs à la meuniere are the best in town. Brunch very popular. Terrine Provencal, roasted lotte and lobster in Sauternes, steak with mixed peppercorns, blueberry crumble cake. $$$$ ♙♙♙

★★★★ **ALISON ON DOMINICK STREET**—38 Dominick Street (near Hudson)—727-1188—Now in its third successful season, this out-of-the-way Soho eatery has nonetheless become a popular destination restaurant, thanks to its indefatigable owner, Alison Price, and talented chef, Thomas Valenti. Alison's is a low-key, but personable restaurant with attractive cream-colored walls, blue banquettes and striking black-and-white photos. Valenti has a sure hand with seasonings. Provencal tart, goat cheese Napoleon, gnocchi with broccoli di rape, skate with cabbage and bacon, squab with lentils, roasted pork loin, trio of chocolate desserts. $$$$ ♙♙♙

★★ **ABYSSINIA**—35 Grand Street (near West Broadway)—226-5959—Very dreary, but one of a handful of Ethiopian restaurants in town. You will squat on stools and must be given a lesson in African etiquette, but it's fun and the spicy food is very interesting. Yemesir ki, doro wat, yasa wot, zegeni. $$$ ♙

★½ **JOUR ET NUIT**—227 West Broadway (at Grand Street)—925-5971—Once you finally get a reservation here, you might wonder what the fuss was all about. Nevertheless, this downtown bistro serving simple French fare remains a highly popular destination, especially among a nocturnal crowd clad in black. Potato chèvre, onglet, leg of lamb, grilled salmon, crème brûlée. $$$ 🍷

★★ **BAROLO**—398 West Broadway (between Spring and Broome Streets)—226-1102—A striking example of contemporary Milanese design, this handsome, three-tiered restaurant also boasts a large garden for summer dining. The kitchen does not match the deftness of the interior design, but you can count on passable pastas and other staples like polenta with mushrooms, fegato Veneziana, and fish soup. Service may be agonizingly slow. $$$ 🍷🍷🍷

★★★ **CAFÉ**—210 Spring Street (near Sixth Avenue)—274-0505—The grandson of Pablo Picasso, Richard Widmaier-Picasso, debuted what could easily have been just another fashionable spot; instead, he has created a place where you'll also find fine food with lots of flair. There's a lively front dining room and a more comfortable "library" in back. Curried chicken soup, salad with roquefort and walnuts, vegetable terrine, lamb sausage with white beans, coq au vin, medallions of sweetbreads, cold hazelnut terrine, yogurt sauce, nougat ice cream, fig tart. $$$ 🍷🍷🍷

★★ **VUCCIRIA**—422 West Broadway (between Prince and Spring)—941-5811—A sibling of uptown Azzuro, with an interior design that resembles a stage set—sort of a building within a building. Original, but it doesn't altogether work. The kitchen's output runs along similar lines; creative in intent, a tad better than average in execution. Pasta with funghi, sautéed baby artichoke, chicken with sausage, stuffed rolled veal breast, tiramisu. Amex only. $$$ 🍷🍷🍷

★ **AMICI MIEI**—475 West Broadway (near Houston Street)—533-1933—Popular and moderately priced (with outdoor dining in summer), this Italian trattoria attracts a somewhat boisterous crowd (a decibel condition that is only worsened by piped-in rock music).

All this could be forgiven if only the food were as rousing as the atmosphere. Caesar salad, carpaccio, calamari and breaded veal chop were all disappointing. Nice wine list, however. $$$ 🍷🍷🍷

★★★ **CAN**—482 West Broadway (corner Houston Street)—533-6333—A striking new arrival to SoHo, with a highly polished, sleek interior, Can serves up Franco-Vietnamese fare of a very high order. Spring roll with lobster, pork dumplings, rice crêpe with blue prawns, apple in fillo pastry with hazelnut ice cream. Perhaps because it is priced somewhat above other area haunts, Can has been slow to take off. Thus it remains an undiscovered but well deserved neighborhood gem. $$$½ 🍷🍷

★★ **MEZZOGIORNO**—195 Spring Street (at Sullivan)—334-2112—A long sliver of a space with festive dioramas for decoration. Good light Italian fare, though somewhat pricey, given the casual environs. Warm mozzarella with mushrooms and string beans, insalata mezzogiorno, carpaccio Harry's Bar, excellent pizzas, risotto with vegetables. No credit cards. $$$ 🍷🍷

★★ **RAOUL'S**—180 Prince Street (at Sullivan Street)—966-3518—One of New York's most atmospheric French bistros, replete with the sights, sounds and flavors of Paris' Boulevard St. Michel. The menu is full of traditional offerings such as leeks vinaigrette, steak au poivre, grilled salmon, profiteroles—all nicely executed, but without tremendous flair. $$$$ 🍷🍷

★★★½ **PROVENCE**—38 MacDougal Street (near Prince Street)—475-7500—A lively and authentic looking bistro of the kind that dot the Riviera, this little spot has become very popular for its unprepossessing decor, its fair prices and its commendable provençal food, especially dishes like pissaladière, brandade and bourride. You can also count on the likes of eggplant terrine, poulet roti, and addicting frites. The early crowd at dinner consists of locals, the later arrivals more of an artsy-literary mix. The front room has more charm than the rear. Closed Monday. Amex only. $$$ 🍷🍷🍷

★★ **VILLA MOSCONI**—69 MacDougal Street (near Houston)—673-0390—A nice, old-fashioned Greenwich Village restaurant of a kind they don't make any more. You come here to eat heartily at a fair price, to be treated like an old friend by owner Peter Mosconi, and to get a good feeling for the way the village used to be a decade or more ago. Suggested dishes are tagliatelle al pesto, seafood stew, veal alla giardinera. $$$ 🍷

★★½ **SOHO KITCHEN AND BAR**—103 Greene Street (near Prince Street)—925-1866—Enormous brick dining room serving good pizzas, pastas, and simple grilled fare. But the real draw is more than 100 wines available by the glass and 21 extraordinary taster's "flights" of eight wines each, poured in 1.5 ounce servings, which range from French country wines to international chardonnays and Chilean cabernet sauvignons. Clearly NYC's best wine bar. $$½ 🍷🍷🍷

★★½ **JERRY'S**—101 Prince Street (between Mercer and Greene)—966-9464—The decor is updated diner, and the ambience very relaxed. But the kitchen is anything but laid back in its diligent preparation of American specialties. Duck breast and duck sausage salad, spinach salad with Swedish bacon, grilled swordfish with cucumber tomato raita, and wholesome sandwiches. Excellent frites. $$½ 🍷

★★ **SAVOY**—70 Prince Street (near Broadway)—219-8570—A diminutive (45 seat) spot with a casual, contemporary feel serving up faintly Mediterranean fare, which is more innovative than it is flavorful. Appetizers such as grilled sardines with red wine and simmered onions, salt cod salad, salad with thyme-baked beets, frek and croutons, entrées such as roast chicken with dry fava bean and green olive stew, roasted skate with salad and shrimp oil vinaigrette, grilled lamb chops with red pepper and eggplant relish all suffer somewhat from underseasoning. Very good plum tart. $$½ 🍷🍷🍷

★½ **L'AUBINIERE**—218 Lafayette Street (near Spring Street)—274-1522—Can something be overly minimally designed? If it can, then you get a sense of

L'Aubiniere, a large terra-cotta-colored dining room with recessed lights and a long bar. It's supposed to be SoHo hip, but it hasn't caused much of a stir, perhaps because the French food is good but not terrific, sometimes bland, mostly okay. Desserts are better than what precedes them. $$$$ 🍷

★★ **ONDA**—430 Broome Street (corner Crosby)—925-4743—Len Allison and Karen Hubert's latest creation is a dramatic departure in form and content from Huberts, their stylish Park Avenue restaurant which closed last year. Onda offers an amalgam of Italian, Indonesian, and Chinese cooking in very casual surroundings. Spring roll, deep-fried oysters, pork saté, veal shank with onion sauce, roasted squab. $$$ 🍷

★½ **BENITO'S II**—163 Mulberry Street (between Grand and Broome Streets)—226-9012—There are so many restaurants in Little Italy that pack them in and turn them out, it's nice to be able to make a reservation at Benito's II, enjoy fresh-made tomato sauce on pasta, garlicky chicken, and the strolling guitarist (he's not all that talented but he's fun). This is a good, if undistinguished, spot to soak up the Little Italy atmosphere. Benito's I right across the street apparently has nothing to do with Benito's II. $$½ 🍷

★★ **ANGELO'S**—146 Mulberry Street (near Grand Street)—966-1277—A very old-fashioned Italian-American spot smack in Little Italy and certainly better than most of the tourist traps that surround it. This place has a homey feel, with its simple decor and black-and-white tile floors, and is as good as you'll find in the neighborhood. Go with the whole family. Perciatelli with a vegetable sauce, chicken with garlic. Closed Mon. $$$ 🍷

★★ **FERRARA**—195 Grand Street (at Mulberry Street)—226-6150—If you wish to get a good aroma of what Little Italy is all about, walk into Ferrara and get a whiff of the freshly brewed espresso and cappuccino, then sit at one of the little tables and have yourself a cannoli—a crisp pastry filled with cream—or a sfogliatelle, flakey pastry with a custard-like cream. This is an authentic Southern Italian café. $

★ **IL CORTILE**—125 Mulberry Street (near Hester Street)—226-6060—This used to be Little Italy's best restaurant, but we've found it has been coasting sideways at best and downwards when it comes to the amenities and service. The food can still be good, but there's a lot better to be had uptown, so why put up with surly waiters who really don't care what you order anyhow? Wine list is no credit either. $$$$ ♉

★★ **WONG KEE**—113 Mott Street (near Canal Street)—226-9018—Here is a clean bright and completely uncluttered Chinese restaurant with the added virtue of being consistent and dependable, which most Chinatown restaurants are not. It's a cliché to say you should order what the Orientals are ordering, but here it is true: look around you and ask for those things that everybody seems to be eating that day. Duck with star anise, beef with sour cabbage. No credit cards. $$

★★½ **SILVER PALACE**—52 Bowery (near Canal Street)—964-1204—A vast hall (with entertainment on Sundays featuring Chinese performers) where waiters rush about with trays full of dim sum dumplings, this is a great place to go for a weekend lunch. They serve all day and the crowds are a fun-loving bunch. Everyone laughs and orders too much, but the spirit is infectious and the dumpling trays irresistible. You pay by the plate, so you'll find it difficult to spend more than $20 per person here. At night they switch to a more conventional, more expensive format. $$½

★★★ **SIU LAM KUNG**—18 Elizabeth Street (near Canal Street)—732-0974—This is one of Chinatown's better Cantonese restaurants, but be sure to make it clear you want the chef's specialties. These would include shrimp-stuffed bean curd, the bird's nest soup, the steamed flounder with ginger, and the braised duck with star anise. The premises are noisy but bright, and you may have to share a table. You do get a good sense of place and of the timeless rush that characterizes all that goes on in Chinatown. $$½

★★ **H.S.F.**—46 Bowery (near Canal Street)—374-1319—Always crowded dim sum restaurant (with a branch in Bridgehampton), serving up a panoply of Cantonese dumplings. Very inexpensive for many dishes which you choose from trays. $$

★★ **NOODLE TOWN**—28½ Bowery (near Canal Street)—349-0923—The name is not encouraging and the place is not much to look at, but this Chinatown noodle parlor serves up fabulous Hong Kong style fare at very low prices ($8.50 for a half duck is the top price on the menu). Don't miss the wide Hong Kong noodles with beef, the duck and dumpling soup, or the pan-fried noodles with black beans. No credit cards. $$

★★½ **KWONG AND WONG**—11 Division Street—(near East Broadway and Bowery)—941-7411—A no-frills seafood house in Chinatown with very fresh fish. It should be: it swims in a tank in the window where you pick out your dinner and they cook it for you in minutes. English is definitely a second language here, but make it clear you want the evening's specials, like geoduck clams and other delicacies. $$$

★★½ **KATZ'S DELICATESSEN**—205 East Houston Street (near Orchard Street)—254-2246—If you want to get to know what a real NYC deli is like, this is your place—a longstanding favorite of New Yorkers who like to shop for bargains on adjacent Orchard Street and then repair to Katz's for big fat sandwiches of steaming tongue, brisket of beef, and corned beef, garlicky frankfurters, dripping pickles, greasy fries, and a bottle of cream soda, served cafeteria style. You've got to move fast and know what you want, because the counter men can make a sandwich faster than you can say, "pastrami-on-rye." Amex only. $½

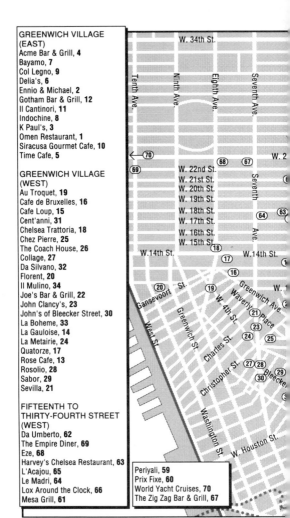

GREENWICH VILLAGE (EAST)
Acme Bar & Grill, **4**
Bayamo, **7**
Col Legno, **9**
Delia's, **6**
Ennio & Michael, **2**
Gotham Bar & Grill, **12**
Il Cantinori, **11**
Indochine, **8**
K Paul's, **3**
Omen Restaurant, **1**
Siracusa Gourmet Cafe, **10**
Time Cafe, **5**

GREENWICH VILLAGE (WEST)
Au Troquet, **19**
Cafe de Bruxelles, **16**
Cafe Loup, **15**
Cent'anni, **31**
Chelsea Trattoria, **18**
Chez Pierre, **25**
The Coach House, **26**
Collage, **27**
Da Silvano, **32**
Florent, **20**
Il Mulino, **34**
Joe's Bar & Grill, **22**
John Clancy's, **23**
John's of Bleecker Street, **30**
La Boheme, **33**
La Gauloise, **14**
La Metairie, **24**
Quatorze, **17**
Rose Cafe, **13**
Rosolio, **28**
Sabor, **29**
Sevilla, **21**

FIFTEENTH TO THIRTY-FOURTH STREET (WEST)
Da Umberto, **62**
The Empire Diner, **69**
Eze, **68**
Harvey's Chelsea Restaurant, **63**
L'Acajou, **65**
Le Madri, **64**
Lox Around the Clock, **66**
Mesa Grill, **61**

Periyali, **59**
Prix Fixe, **60**
World Yacht Cruises, **70**
The Zig Zag Bar & Grill, **67**

W. 34th St.

Tenth Ave.
Ninth Ave.
Eighth Ave.
Seventh Ave.

W. 2

W. 22nd St.
W. 21st St.
W. 20th St.
W. 19th St.
W. 18th St.
W. 17th St.
W. 16th St.
W. 15th St.

Seventh Ave.

W.14th St.

Gansevoort St.

West St.

Greenwich St.

W. 4th St.

Greenwich Ave.

Waverly Place

Charles St.

Christopher St.

Bleecker

Washington St.

W. Houston St.

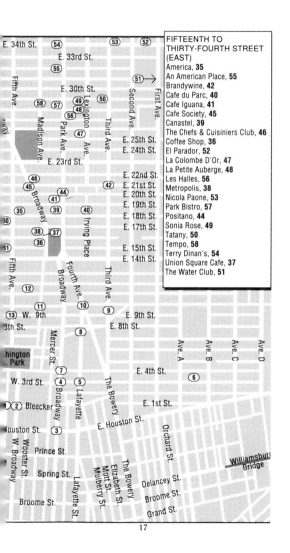

GREENWICH VILLAGE (EAST)

★★ **OMEN RESTAURANT**—113 Thompson Street (near Bleecker)—925-8923—This casual and inviting country-style Japanese restaurant boasts an original and well executed menu. An effective use of wood paneling creates a serene atmosphere. You'll find traditional dishes like tuna sashimi and mixed tempura, along with innovative preparations such as tuna steak with ginger, or spinach and scallops with peanut cream. Try the house saké. $$$ 🍷

★★★ **ENNIO & MICHAEL**—539 LaGuardia Place (near Bleecker Street)—677-8577—Two Abruzzese owners run this charming, sprightly Village place serving robust and zesty Italian food at a fair price. Very popular with locals. Zucchini fritti, insalata di mare, gnocchi in tomato sauce, shrimp fra diavolo. Amex only. Closed Monday. $$$½ 🍷🍷

★½ **K PAUL'S**—622 Broadway (near Houston)—460-9633—Some concepts simply don't travel. Crowds may line New Orlean's Chartres Street to sample super-chef Paul Prudhomme's Cajun fare, but the "bull-pen" he has constructed to accommodate New Yorkers waiting for a table—while an enormous service bar is off-limits—simply won't do. Other "democratic" approaches to dining—community tables and service are equally foreign. Only the ultra-friendly staff, and an evening dance ritual known as the second line—warm up the otherwise cold interior. When Prudhomme is in residence the food may shine. But otherwise, gumbos, Cajun popcorn, even signature dishes like blackened prime rib and blackened yellowfin tuna fail to excite. The printed wine list consists of two entries: a red and a white. Try and tackle the 10 oz. cajun martini instead. Closed Saturday. Dinner only. $$$$ 🍷

★★ **ACME BAR & GRILL**—9 Great Jones Street (near Broadway)—420-1934—An authentic, down-home Cajun joint, replete with corrugated tin ceilings, exposed beams and every conceivable bottle of hot sauce ever produced lining an enormous interior wall. Oyster Po-Boys, (deep-fried) Cajun shrimp, brown rice and greens are just a few of the regional specialties offered at this casual, inexpensive, forever lively Louisiana transplant. No credit cards. $$ ♀

★ **TIME CAFE**—380 Lafayette Street (near Great Jones Street)—533-7000—Talk about an "attitude"! This place, run by a former disco door manager, is supposed to be a kinder, gentler restaurant for the '90s, with an announced bias on the eco-system curve. You are received by a bored young hostess who seems terribly distressed you've shown up. The staff is surprisingly shabbily dressed. The noise level is absolutely deafening. And the place looks like a lunch room. If you can stand all this, the food's passable—an amalgam of pastas, pizzas, grilled chicken—oh, you know the menu by heart. $$$ ♀

★★ **DELIA'S**—197 East 3rd Street (between Avenues A and B)—254-9184—Located smack in the heart of alphabet-city, Delia's nonetheless attracts a very eclectic crowd. You are wise to come by car, or at least to pre-arrange a pick-up by taxi or limo, since this is not a neighborhood where after-dinner strolls are recommended. Once inside, you are transported into an imaginative and alluring environment, redolent of a night club in London's Soho. The fare is simple but good: onion tarte, salmon mousse, steak au poivre. Double chocolate cake. Dancing to a retro beat. Dinner only. Private parties Sunday and Monday. $$$ ♀♀

★★ **BAYAMO**—704 Broadway (near 4th Street)—475-5151—Named after a Cuban town settled by a Chinese contingent, Bayamo serves specialties that are a blend of both cultures. Won ton fritos (stuffed with chorizo), stir-fried duckling with black beans and chiles, Cuban sandwiches, corn crust pizzas. Upbeat decor, casual. $$ ♀

★★ **INDOCHINE**—430 Lafayette Street (near Astor Place)—505-5111—Tucked away opposite the Public Theater is this exotic Vietnamese eatery, complete with a banana-leaf motif on its walls. Convenient as it is for theater-goers, Indochine has developed a certain amount of cachet, and draws an interesting crowd from all over town. Good shrimp beignets, marinated beef salad, and chicken wings. Dinner only. $$$ 🍴

★★½ **COL LEGNO**—231 East 9th Street (near Third Avenue)—777-4650—A sparse and unassuming trattoria—such as one might find in a small Tuscan town—with a very capable kitchen. Seven splendid offerings from the brick pizza oven include standards like The Margherita and less conventional combinations like The Carolyna (artichoke sauce and fresh tomato). Good homemade pasta (try the tagliarini col pesto) and satisfying grilled preparations; for an overview of the kitchen's output, try the grigliata misto—chicken, quail and sweet sausage. Good tiramisu. $$$ 🍴

★★★ **SIRACUSA GOURMET CAFE**—65 Fourth Avenue (near 10th Street)—254-1940—Although the setting here is friendly and ultra-simple, there is nothing facile about the cuisine at this popular little Village haunt. Ignore the nondescript decor and focus instead on the menu; an enticing array of antipasti—fried vegetables, superb charcuterie—and excellent pastas such as ravioli stuffed with eggplant and pignoli nuts, taglierini with sausage and tomato. There is a take-out counter up front featuring many of the menu highlights and wonderful biscotti to go. $$$ 🍴

★★ **IL CANTINORI**—32 East 10th Street (near University Place)—673-6044—Perhaps the strain of running two other restaurants (Aureole and Periyali) has caused the owners to neglect this one. Everything is off here—starting with the voice on the phone which makes you feel unwanted when you call for a reservation. The sauces need seasoning, the pasta clings together, the lemon tart tastes like aluminum, the waiters seem bored, and the wine list is way over-priced. Still, you can get unusual Tuscan dishes here, portions are generous and food prices fair. Pasta with lamb ragu, carré of veal with whipped potatoes, and biscotti with vin santo. $$$$ 🍴🍴🍴

★★★★★ **GOTHAM BAR AND GRILL**—12 East 12th Street (between Fifth Avenue and University Place)—620-4020—A true Manhattan destination, brilliantly presided over by Chef Alfred Portale and co-owner

Jerry Kretchmer. This vast, strikingly-designed dining room (complete with Statue of Liberty) serves as a vibrant and cosmopolitan setting for serious eaters who demand and get the best the kitchen has to offer. Portale is soaring: His sense of balance and textures together with flawless technique (he studied with Michel Guèrard and Jacques Maximin) shows in every dish and nothing is ever overdone or eccentric. Salade frisée, warm skate salad, penne with wild mushrooms, sautéed halibut with endive, grilled loin of rabbit with white beans, yellowfin tuna au poivre, grilled squab with pancetta and new potatoes, profiteroles, flowerless chocolate cake, and hazelnut apple tart with cinnamon ice cream. $$$$½ ♙♙♙♙

GREENWICH VILLAGE (WEST)

★★ ROSE CAFE—24 Fifth Avenue (at Ninth Street)—260-4118—After his departure from Melrose, chef Richard Krause took over this thought-to-be-jinxed location. By dropping prices and offering good value, he truly made a silk purse from a sow's ear. The food is commendable, if not enthralling (avoid all the pastas), and much of it has a California style to it. The staff is efficient, but such slovenly dress doesn't do much for the appetite. Salad of pears with gorgonzola and potato, loin of lamb with oregano brown butter, veal chop with sorrel cream. $$$ ♙

★★½ LA GAULOISE—502 Avenue of the Americas (near 13th Street)—691-1363—A very affable neighborhood bistro with dark wood paneling and mirrors in the style of art nouveau, that serves up serious bistro fare. Good hors d'oeuvres variés, salad frisée, rabbit forrestière, skate wings, sweet and sour sweetbreads, plum tarte. Service is friendly, but can be quite slow. Nice wine list. $$$ ♙♙

★★½ CAFE LOUP—105 West 13th Street (near Avenue of the Americas)—255-4746—This is a casual and inviting Village restaurant where you can sit down to a full course meal or order from an array of light entrées like pasta or smoked chicken called "small plates." For regular appetites, consider the pâté forestière or carrot soup, followed by delectable roasted chicken and succulent French fries, black bass, raspberry walnut tart. $$$ 🍷

★★ **CAFE DE BRUXELLES**—118 Greenwich Avenue (near 13th Street)—206-1830—Real Village charm, lace curtains, simple appointments, and a menu full of pretty fair Belgian specialties like moules marinières, choucroute de Bruegel, salade aux chicons and waterzooi. The cassoulet and carbonnade flamande are not up to par though. The raspberry tart is recommendable. Open Sunday. $$$ 🍷

★★★½ **QUATORZE**—240 West 14th Street (between Seventh and Eighth Avenues)—206-7006—An attractive French bistro (owned by another Peter Meltzer, not the co-author of PASSPORT TO NEW YORK RESTAURANTS), loosely modeled on Paris's celebrated Brasserie Lipp, which is verging on institutional status in its own right. Though the location lacks the clan of the Boulevard St. Germain, staples such as saucisson chaud, salade aux lardons, creamy pâté, coq au vin, calf's liver and choucroute garni are worthy of the real thing. Excellent frites. One of the best apple tarts in the city. Amex only. $$$ 🍷🍷

★★★ **CHELSEA TRATTORIA**—108 Eighth Avenue (near 15th Street)—924-7786—Freshness, fairness of price, and conviviality mark this unpretentious, constantly packed trattoria ignored by most of the food press. The Bitici Brothers have everything down pat here, from the delicious Florentine bean soup to the seafood al cartoccio and creamy tiramisu. There is a tendency to oversalt some dishes, and the captains can be remiss, but this is a wonderful little spot not too hard on the budget. $$$$ 🍷🍷

★★★ **AU TROQUET**—328 West 12th Street—(near West 4th Street)—924-3413—A charming French bistro located on the western perimeter of the Village. The place is evocative of a romantic, old-world, country hideaway, replete with lace curtains and bric-a-brac. Delectable seafood pâte, vegetable terrine, roast chicken, salmon and spinach en croute. Good wine list. Closed Sunday. Dinner only. $$$ 🍷

★½ **FLORENT**—69 Gansevoort Street (near Greenwich Street)—989-5779—Absolutely, positively the hippest restaurant in lower Manhattan, not for its food—just passable French bistro fare—but for the retro neighborhood it's in (the meat market district), the decor (barely converted diner), and the late-night crowd that includes Madonna, the Talking Heads, and a lot of other musicians. The waiters are friendly and, if you can get a table after nine o'clock, you can just inhale the atmosphere and have a good time. Pre-arrange a return taxi or limo (open 24 hours). No credit cards. $$½ ☙

★★★ **SEVILLA**—62 Charles Street (near Seventh Avenue)—243-9513—A bustling and spirited Spanish restaurant, heavy on wood paneling and pleasantly informal in nature, catering to a somewhat youthful crowd. Traditional menu, replete with grilled chorizo, Spanish ham and olives, mariscada with green sauce, paella Valenciana with lobster, is both fresh and deftly prepared. What's more, most entrées fall under the $16 range, making this an excellent spot for diners in search of good fun, good quality, and good value. $$$ ☙

★★ **JOE'S BAR & GRILL**—142 West 10th Street (between Avenue of the Americas and Seventh Avenue)—727-1785—A cozy, brick-walled spot where you can count on an enthusiastic greeting and such nursery perfect dishes as Caesar salad prepared at table-side, filet mignon with béarnaise sauce, meat loaf with creamed spinach. $$$ ☙☙

★★ **JOHN CLANCY'S**—181 West 10th Street (near Seventh Avenue)—691-0551—A serious, perhaps too seriously taken fish restaurant that is overly expensive for the rather simply prepared fare. Lobster bisque, sesame shrimp won tons, seared yellowfin tuna, halibut with roasted garlic sauce, mahi mahi with sun-dried tomato relish. $$$$ ☙☙☙

★★★½ **LA METAIRIE**—189 West 10th Street (corner West 4th Street near Seventh Avenue)—989-0343—Now that owner Sylvain Fareri has severed ties with his uptown establishment, he is devoting all his time to this informal space—and it shows. Enlivened and considerably enlarged, it still bares quaint touches of the Provence countryside, and the menu is rich in regional influences. Carrot and mint soup, boudin de fruits de mer, quail stuffed with foie gras and spinach in a black truffle sauce, baby squid with tomatoes, herb roasted cornish hen, crème brûlée royale. $$$ ♉♉♉

★★ **CHEZ PIERRE**—170 Waverly Place (Near Christopher Street)—929-7194—A boisterous and cramped little bistro (located in a landmark 1820's building) that instantly evokes memories of Paris (even the waiters are bossy) and can be very amusing if the mood strikes right. Decent onion soup, goat cheese salad, good rumpsteak au poivre. No credit cards. $$$ ♉♉

Ŏ ★★★★★ **THE COACH HOUSE**—110 Waverly Place (near Avenue of the Americas)—777-0303—Ever since Leon Lianides opened the Coach House in 1949, American cooking has never had higher standards to meet than those set here. The premises are exquisitely set with antiques and fine paintings on wood-paneled walls (this was once John Wanamaker's coach house). As Frank Conroy notes in his novel *Prince of Tides,* the Coach House puts you in touch with New York's unique greatness. You can't go wrong with anything on the menu, from the cornsticks to the famous black bean soup. Rack of lamb, bass in bouillon, steak au poivre, quince tart, dacquoise. $$$$ ♉♉♉

★★½ **COLLAGE**—314 Bleecker Street (near Grove Street)—645-1612—A kaleidoscope of striking images creates a lively backdrop for this Americanized bistro presided over by photographer Patrick Demarchelier. You'll find good leeks vinaigrette, saucisse aux choux braisés, mussels and cajun catfish, grilled chicken with frites. Good profiteroles. Very reasonable. $$½ ♉♉

★★½ **ROSOLIO**—11 Barrow Street (near Seventh Avenue)—645-9224—This trattoria, run by the exuberant Teresa is stark but quite warm (and very loud) with mottled walls, high ceiling and terrazzo floors. The food can be delicious or mundane depending on your choice. The wine list is modest but well chosen. The staff is not. Crostini di polenta, stracci with duck, tiramisu. Dinner only. $$$½ ♛♛

★★ **SABOR**—20 Cornelia Street (near Bleecker Street)—243-9579—For years this has been downtown's best little Cuban restaurant, run without pomp or trendiness, and always busy. It's a very small storefront, and the food is spicy, good and served with largesse. Empanadas filled with chorizo, baked snapper with garlic and lime juice, carne estofada, salted codfish in tomato sauce, Key lime pie. $$½ ♛

★★½ **JOHN'S OF BLEECKER STREET**—278 Bleecker Street (near Seventh Avenue)—243-1680— Along with Mario's in the Bronx (q.v.) John's make the best traditional Neapolitan pizzas in New York, with a good crisp crust, neither too thick or too thin, freshly made sauces, good cheese, and a baking process that makes all the difference. This is the Promised Land for great pie. No credit cards. $ ♛

★★★ **CENT'ANNI**—50 Carmine Street (near Bleecker Street)—989-9494—A very lively, casual, family-style trattoria nestled in the heart of the Village, which attracts diners from all over the city. Sautéed fava beans, baby roast pheasant, pasta specials such as tortellini with prosciutto and peas in a cream sauce, roasted peppers with anchovies, calamari, veal chop. Reasonable wine list. $$$ ♛♛♛

★★★ **DA SILVANO**—260 Avenue of the Americas (near Bleecker Street)—982-2343—Attractive, exposed brick interior. This place caters to an informal yet fashionable clientele who comes here for the crostini, cannelloni, spaghetti alla puttanesca, and a host of specials. Amex only. $$$$½ ♛♛♛

★★ **LA BOHEME**—24 Minetta Lane (near Avenue of the Americas and Bleecker)—473-6447—A gem of a bistro, tucked away in an alley beside the Minetta Lane Theater. Superb appetizer pizzas with artichoke or escargot toppings. Roasted chicken, and steak au poivre are well-prepared, but do not achieve the same heights. Modest, well-chosen wine list. Innovative interior by design wizard Sam Lopata.

Lunch Sundays only. Amex only. $$$ 🍷

★★½ **IL MULINO**—86 West 3rd Street (near MacDougal Street)—673-3783—An Abruzzese heritage gives this lively, very popular trattoria a real snap, and the food is robust and full of flavor. The premises are very cramped for the size of the crowd that inundates the place, and the unending crush at the bar keeps this from being an entirely pleasant experience. All the pastas are superb, especially those with seafood. Also, the veal chop is one of the best in town. $$$$ 🍷🍷

FIFTEENTH TO
THIRTY-FOURTH STREET (EAST)

★★ **COFFEE SHOP**—16th Street and Union Square West—243-7969—A retro hot spot with a young crowd, pretty waitresses and a barrier at the door to keep out the overflow. The place is owned by models and looks it—all flash and glitter, but overall, kind of fun too—until around midnight when the place becomes unbearably crowded and noisy. The quasi-Brazilian fare, which is decently priced, is pretty tasty—cheese muffins, coconut batter shrimp, excellent roast chicken with wonderful mashed potatoes, yummy creamed spinach, a very well-made Cuban sandwich, and guava crepes for dessert. Very casual dress advised. Open 24 hours. $$½ 🍷

★★ **METROPOLIS**—310 Union Square West (near 16th Street)—675-2300—A cheerily renovated neoclassical structure that now features a spate of grilled fare, faintly California in feel. This is a very lively (and as the evening transpires, increasingly noisy) and informal place to dine. Avoid the more ambitious dishes like sautéed camembert wrapped in bacon with honey sauce. Shiitake mushroom and vegetable "carpaccio" salad, sundried tomato ravioli, grilled free range chicken, seared yellowfin tuna with soy, lime and sesame oil. Dessert list accompanied by appropriate after-dinner wines. $$$ 🍷🍷🍷

★★★★½ **UNION SQUARE CAFE**—21 East 16th Street (between Fifth Avenue and Union Square West)—

243-4020—A highly popular and attractive down-town setting, scene of animated dining and many a special wine and food gala. Owner Danny Meyer never rests on his laurels, and chef Michael Romano's innovative touches make this kitchen one of Manhattan's finest. Oysters Union Square remain a signature appetizer, but don't ignore the baked goat cheese and flageolet salad, the fagioli alla Toscana or the bombolotti al modo mio with sweet fennel sausage. A side dish of hot garlic potato chips is another must. You can count on delectable beef and lamb, herb roasted chicken with polenta, roasted loin of rabbit, and grilled marinated tuna. There are also nightly pasta specials worth considering, such as penne with sausage. The wine list is most innovative with a good selection by the glass. Now open for Sunday dinner. $$$ 🍷🍷🍷🍷🍷

★ **AMERICA**—9 East 18th Street (near Fifth Avenue)—505-2110—A cavernous and lively muralled eatery that tends to attract a youngish crowd. Many are content to hang out at the enormous and inviting bar and simply watch the scene. Noise levels can be problematic. Not surprisingly, America serves up an ambitious but often inconsistent array of American favorites and specials, from po' boy sandwiches to burgers and fajitas. $$½ 🍷🍷

★ **CANASTEL**—229 Park Avenue South (near 19th Street)—677-9622—A founding member of the cavernous, columned, Hi-Tech, neon, Italianate restaurant set—with a clientele to match the decor. A formula restaurant with a formula menu. The best addition to an otherwise bland menu is the artfully executed brick oven pizza. Fairly priced wine list. $$$½ 🍷🍷

★★★ **CAFE DU PARC**—106 East 19th Street (near Lexington Avenue)—777-7840—Cozy, though somewhat mismatched decor, nestled a stone's throw from Gramercy Park. Traditional French fare includes duck sausage, grilled veal, grilled salmon and roasted calf's liver. Closed Sunday. $24.95 Pre-theater dinner. $$ 🍷

★★ **CAFE IGUANA**—235 Park Avenue South (at 19th

27

Street)—529-4770—A big, sprawling bar-restaurant packed tight with singles, vibrating with music, and as fast-paced as a road runner, this is a very gregarious Mexican eatery (complete with t-shirts for sale) with above-average food and terrific "Iguana-rita" cocktails. The fajitas and chicken Tijuana are also recommended. Good Sunday brunch and a nice spot to take kids earlier in the evening. $$$ ♟

★★ **POSITANO**—250 Park Avenue (at 20th Street)—777-6211—Much of the trendy crowds have retreated from this airy, comfortable, and, at night, romantic Italian restaurant, and so, too, has much of the flavor that once distinguished the cooking here, which tastes as if they are cutting corners with ingredients and just going through the motions in the kitchen. The menu reads much better than it tastes. Nonetheless, a pleasant spot for a business lunch in the area. $$$½ ♟♟♟

★ **CAFE SOCIETY**—915 Broadway (at 21st Street)—529-8282—There's nothing that extraordinary about the fare served at this cavernous, rose-hued, column-festooned cantina. The real attraction here, as the name clearly suggests, is the crowd scene; has been one of the hottest spots to mingle in Manhattan, although its popularity has started to dwindle. $$$ ♟

★★ **BRANDYWINE**—274 Third Avenue (near 21st Street)—353-8190—No longer serving its signature Alsatian dishes, Brandywine nevertheless remains a pleasant enough spot for lunch or dinner in an otherwise barren sector of Third Avenue. The atmosphere is clubby and comfortable. But the kitchen's accent is now strictly continental (the owners always offered an alternative menu to spatzle and choucroute), though somewhat heavy on beef. You'll also find a well rounded wine list. $$$ ♟♟♟♟

★★½ **THE CHEFS CUISINIERS CLUB**—36 East 22nd Street (off Broadway)—228-4399—"CCC," as it's called, is a worthwhile idea well realized: Several of NYC's most notable chefs, e.g., Rick Moonen of The Water Club, Charles Palmer of Aureole, et al, opened this pleasant little bistro as an after-service refuge where confrères can get together to eat, swap stories

28

and blow off steam. The public is also welcome to enjoy chef Peter Assue's restrained Mediterranean food, which is a bit under-seasoned but very tasty. The premises are spare, the bluejeans on the waiters are slovenly and the wine list is minimal, but this is a good neighborhood spot and cannot help but intrigue those who follow the comings-and-goings of New York City's stellar chefs. $$$ ☙

★★★½ **LA COLOMBE D'OR**—134 East 26th Street (near Lexington Avenue)—689-0666—For years this cozy and casual spot has been a paragon French bistro serving up good French food under the supervision of owners George and Helen Studley. Now that Naj Zougari, a former sous chef under Gray Kunz at Adrienne, is firmly ensconced in the kitchen, it's not impossible that classics from his native Tangiers may one day appear on the menu. For the moment, however, it remains trés français: ragoût of escargots with white beans, crèpe with ratatouille, seared sea scallops, grilled herbed chicken breast, grilled duck, flourless chocolate cake. $$$½ ☙☙☙

★★½ **LA PETITE AUBERGE**—116 Lexington Avenue (near 28th Street)—689-5003—For a dozen years this has been one of the more dependable East Side bistros very much in the Parisian mold—simply decorated with dark woods and beams—the kind of place you make your own if you live in the neighborhood. The menu is full of clichés but the food can be delicious—yummy old-fashioned coquilles St.-Jacques, pink leg of lamb with flageolets, perfect soufflé au Grand Marnier and excellent frites. $$$$ ☙

★★½ **LES HALLES**—411 Park Avenue South (near 28th Street)—679-4111—The owners of Park Bistro across the street also run this amiable, loud replication of a Parisian butcher shop-restaurant, and it's not a place for those who eat oat bran for breakfast. This is a carnivore's dream—hanger steak, cassoulet, French fries, and all sorts of fat-rich, absolutely delicious bourgeois dishes, including some exemplary fruit tarts. Service is hectic, the place is always packed, so expect a wait for your table. The wine list has some interesting country bottlings. $$$½ ☙

★★★★ **PARK BISTRO**—414 Park Avenue South (near 28th Street)—689-1360—In look and in feel, this is one of the best approximations of a French bistro in Manhattan. Leather banquettes, posters and photographs create the right ambience. Indeed, Owners Philippe Lajaunie, Max Bernard and Jean-Michel Diot run a sprightly dining room, popular as much for its charm as for its food. Chef Diot's Provence-inspired cooking is a delight. Be sure to sample their signature appetizer consisting of potato slices smothered with grilled goat cheese, radicchio, and an olive vinaigrette dressing. Mackerel and fennel salad, shellfish soup and mussel soup are all worthwhile. For a main course, consider the medallions of beef in a red wine sauce, rabbit with salsify, or leg of lamb. Crème brûlée. $$$½ 🍷🍷🍷

★★ **SONIA ROSE**—132 Lexington Avenue (between 28th and 29th Streets)—545-1777—A nice effort in the right direction, Sonia Rose is a small, pleasant slip of a dining room done in gray walls hung with some truly unattractive paintings and black-and-white photos of the owner. The menu is very brief, the portions not enough to fill anyone up, and the concepts fairly derivative. The nearly raw tuna with crushed black peppers and the minuscule slice of Linzer torte are recommendable. $$$$ 🍷🍷

★★ **TATANY**—388 Third Avenue, (near 29th Street)—686-1871—A modest looking Japanese restaurant which has developed a strong following that extends beyond the neighborhood. Sashimi, stir-fried chicken, Tempura. $$ 🍷

★★★ **TEMPO**—30 East 29 Street (near Madison Avenue)—532-8125—A sprightly, if cramped dining room that caters to a business crowd by day and New Yorkers from all over by night. There can be occasional confusion over confirmed reservations. Once seated, you will delight in specials such as pasta with asparagus and sun dried tomatoes or broccoli and sausage, funghi trifolati, red snapper, grilled marinated chicken, and home made Tartufo. Closed Sunday. $$$½ 🍷🍷

★★½ **THE WATER CLUB**—500 East 30th Street (on

the East River)—683-3333—This barge restaurant hasn't the majestic view of its sibling, The River Café, but it has a more handsome interior, with a high ceiling, ships' models and fine banquet facilities. Chef Rick Moonen has a lot of talent, but he seems caught up in volume control—too many customers day in and day out. Read between the lines of the menu and you'll find his best efforts like pan-seared red snapper on a fennel wand with crisp leeks, calf's liver with melted onions and flourless macadamia chocolate cake. The service staff is problematic here, starting at the maitre d's desk, where you're sized up for an appropriate table, which may well be in the smoking section if you don't ask. Dinner can also take a very long time. $$$$ ☗☗

★★★★½ AN AMERICAN PLACE—2 Park Avenue (entrance an 32nd Street)—684-2122—As godfather of the New American Cooking movement and heir to the mantle of James Beard, Larry Forgione has never veered from his belief that American cookery can be among the finest in the world. In his hands it is, especially at his expansive, handsome postmodern quarters. Forgione's menu includes several signature dishes like terrine of three smoked fish, and warm duck sausage with scallion spoonbread griddle cakes. There are delectable appetizers like asparagus with country ham and cheese, peanut barbecued Gulf shrimp, and lobster and wild mushroom croquettes with spicy red pepper sauce. Winning main courses include sautéed breast of free range chicken, sweet potato ravioli with pecan vinaigrette, breast of pheasant with roast peppers and wild mushrooms, adobo duck, lamb chops with fresh mint marinade, and Black Angus beef with potato gorgonzola galette. For dessert, be sure to try the banana Betty, the apple pan dowdy or the peanut butter ice cream sandwich. $$$$ ☗☗☗

★ TERRY DINAN'S—10 Park Avenue (entrance on 34th Street)—576-1010—Supposedly an attempt to bring back the former glory of the "21" Club, this overly bright, badly decorated dining room is run by a former manager of "21" and even has some of the same waiters and kitchen staff. The menu and service are actually an embarrassment, reminding you how poor the "21" kitchen used to be before its renovation in 1987. Except for some plump crab cakes and mushrooms Divan, the food is pretty nondescript, including a school cafeteria version of chicken hash and a club sandwich that didn't even contain tomato! $$$$ ♀

★★ **EL PARADOR**—325 East 34th Street (between First and Second Avenues)—679-6812—For years, sampling Mexican food in Manhattan meant an evening at El Parador. With its stuccoed walls, subdued lighting, and curio-filled bar (that still churns out excellent margaritas), the overall impression is very south of the border, circa 1960. You still dine very well, even though the menu is also somewhat dated. Nachos Royale, chiles rellenos, deep-fried chimichango, taco special. $$½ ♀

★★ **NICOLA PAONE**—207 East 34th Street (near Third Avenue)—889-3239—Ridiculously expensive for this part of town, Nicola Paone once seemed innovative, but it's actually rather tired and going through the motions. An old-fashioned menu full of lasagna, manicotti, and veal Marsala. The trompe l'oeil atmosphere has a certain charm however, and the glass of house wine generous and good. $$$$ ♀♀♀

FIFTEENTH TO
THIRTY-FOURTH STREET (WEST)

★★★ **MESA GRILL**—102 Fifth Avenue (near 15th Street)—807-7400—Owner Jerry Kretchmer (he also co-owns Gotham Bar and Grill, q.v.) has turned the former premises of Sofi into a boisterous, colorful eatery, full of tall columns, artsy photographs, and a good bar area, all quite apt for chef Bobby Flay's exciting Southwest-inspired food. Every dish has lots of flavor, lots of color, and zip. This is a complete package—a pleasing atmosphere, a smart-looking young crowd, and novel cuisine. Very noisy however, especially upstairs. White bean and roasted tomato soup, shrimp tamale, blue corn salmon cakes, grilled swordfish, gingerbread ice cream sandwich, vanilla buñuelo. $$$½ 🍷

★★ **DA UMBERTO**—107 West 17th Street (near 6th Avenue)—989-0303—A highly popular, spirited, and inordinately noisy Italian trattoria with customers lining the bar awaiting confirmed reservations. The menu includes glistening vegetable antipasti, and hearty braised rabbit, but mostly the kitchen does not achieve the same highs as the decibel level. $$$ 🍷

★★★½ **PRIX FIXE**—18 West 18th Street (near Fifth Avenue)—675-6777—The concept is right for the times: Take over the premises of a grand café (most recently Il Palazzo), do it up with style, put a brilliant young chef named Terence Brennan (formerly of the Polo) in the kitchen, and offer menus at $21 and $36, and wines in three price categories. What's amazing is the quality of the food—pretty close to the pricier glories of Gotham Bar and Grill. Volume can take its toll in the way of annoying delays, and excessive noise, but this remains a terrific place to go for fine food at a square price. Skate with pickled vegetables, loin of lamb with mustard broth, ragout of corn and mushrooms with aged, farm goat cheese, rhubarb consommé with mascarpone mousse, fruit consommé with ginger and Champagne. 🍷

○ ★ **HARVEY'S CHELSEA RESTAURANT**—108 West

18th (near Avenue of the Americas)—243-5644—The decor in this turn-of-the-century saloon is almost more appealing than the food; rich Honduras mahogany and brass fixtures adorn a massive bar. One of the few vestiges of Olde New York. The simple American menu is adequate. Amex only. $$ ♀

★★★½ **LE MADRI**—168 West 18th Street (near Seventh Avenue)—727-8022—Still going strong, Le Madri has succeeded not only because of the hype, but also because of its food. Add to this a very beautiful crowd of regulars from the fashion and publishing world, and owner Pino Luongo has the right mix. The gimmick here—backed up with talent—is to bring in regional Italian chefs on a rotating basis. The revolving door policy created brief problems this spring, but now that chef Marta Pulini is in residence, the kitchen is back to normal. The pizzas are terrific, the pastas very authentic and true to the best in Italy, and the steak alla fiorentina is a nonpareil. Don't miss the desserts either. Despite the crush, and, too often, a wait, this is a great spot to go (ideal after shopping at Barney's down the street). Late supper menu after 11:00 PM. $$$$ ♀♀♀

★★ **L'ACAJOU**—53 West 19th Street (near Avenue of the Americas)—645-1706—A pleasant spot which has continued to improve over time. Co-owner Guy Raoul and chef Michael Becker often feature traditional dishes from their native Alsace. In fact, an unbelievable 35 Alsatian wines can be found on their stellar wine list. Escargots in Cognac, steak frites, red snapper with tomatoe fondue, and specials such as choucroute garni, venison grand veneur, and stuffed trout. $$½ ♀♀♀

★★½ **PERIYALI**—35 West 20th Street (near Avenue of the Americas)—463-7890—An enticing Greek restaurant doing some out-of-the-ordinary cooking that clearly appeals to a regular crowd who loves being here. We enjoyed the food, which was nicely seasoned and amply portioned out. If you feel like sampling contemporary Greek cooking, Periyali (which means "Seashore") is the place to go right now. Specialties include wild mushrooms, feta and onion salad, lamb "exotica," grilled shrimp with herbs, salmon in phyllo, and their signature preparation, charcoal grilled octopus, marinated in red wine. Don't overlook the cinnamon ice cream. $$$ 🍷

★★ **LOX AROUND THE CLOCK**—676 Avenue of the Americas (near 21st Street)—691-3535—A highly spirited, somewhat funky joint, heavy on decorative neon and kinetic paint. Recommended: all sandwiches named for after-hours spots such as Palladium, Limelight, etc., containing fillings like lox, cream cheese and onion. Decent pizza, burgers, and even matzoh ball soup. Open 24 hours Thursday through Saturday; until 4:00 AM other nights. $$ 🍷

★★★ **THE EMPIRE DINER**—210 Tenth Avenue (near 22nd Street)—243-2736—There's nothing like it in its category. A restored Deco showpiece, replete with Formica and chrome. Amusing appetizers, eclectic appetizers from hummus and barbecued chicken wings to nachos and wontons. Excellent chili sundae, BLT, blue plate specials. Pianist some nights. Good beer list. Casual. Amex only. $$ 🍷

★½ **THE ZIG ZAG BAR & GRILL**—206 West 23rd Street (near Seventh Avenue)—645-5060—More a bar than a grill, this very gregarious Chelsea establishment hosts a good cross section of NYC's artists, photogs, stylists and other nightcrawlers who come here mainly for the camaraderie but fill up on quite good sandwiches of red peppers and salami, very juicy burgers, and gloppy desserts. Skip the ribs. Amex only. $$ 🍷

★½ **EZE**—254 West 23rd Street (near Eighth Avenue)—691-1140—The unadorned grayness of the interior decor here sets a tone from which even the kitchen never recovers. (You might try reserving in the garden in season to escape the gloom). Despite an impressive track record, chef Gina Zarrilli doesn't quite deliver. Although the greeting here is very friendly, the vaguely provençal food fails to excite. Corsican salad, red snapper couscous, rack of lamb. Dinner only Tues–Sat. $$$$½ 🍷🍷

○ ★★ **WORLD YACHT CRUISES**—Pier 62 at West 23rd Street (on the Hudson River)—929-7090—Nothing quite so special exists anywhere in the world, for the three-hour yacht cruise around Manhattan gives you more spectacle than Windows on the World, the River Café and the Rainbow Room combined. Add to this some above-average continental cuisine, dancing to a good band, and gratuities (but not drinks) all for $59–$64.50. ♀

THIRTY-FIFTH TO FIFTIETH STREET (EAST)

★★ **BIENVENUE**—21 East 36th Street (near Madison)—684-0215—Tidy, cramped, loud. A fine bistro atmosphere makes this a good casual stop for lunch or a quick dinner in the area. Boeuf a la bourguignonne, coq au vin. Closed Sunday. $$½ ♀

★★★ **VIA VIA**—560 Third Avenue (near 38th Street)—573-6093—A lively, retro-looking dining room which draws an attractive crowd and serves up remarkably good Italian fare. Even the carpaccio takes on a special flavor here. Insalata Caprese, calamari inferno, and daily pasta specials. Very good wine list. Uptown branch located at 1294 Third Avenue. $$$ ♀♀

★ **RIO GRANDE**—160 East 38th Street (off Third Avenue)—867-0922—Possibly NYC's most crowded restaurant, with two enormous dining rooms and a patio jammed in warm weather with people sipping wonderful blue margaritas. The appetizers here are very good, but the entrees are mediocre and unexceptional. Deep-fried foods are to be avoided. Nachos, tacos al carbon. $$ ♀

★★★ **SATURNIA**—70 Park Avenue (at 38th Street in the Doral Park Avenue Hotel)—983-3333—Dogmatism in the service of good taste may work with French classicism, but when it comes to so-called spa food, it is usually more of a disservice. Yet chef Derrick Dickers has been able to combine U.S. Dietary Guidelines and the recommendations of the American Heart Association on salt, fat, and cholesterol in food with delectable results. You'll never miss a calorie with cooking this fine, with three-course meals weighing in at less than 700 calories. So have one of his rich, high-fat desserts as a reward. Monkfish with radicchio and red lentils, loin of lamb with white beans, warm apple and blueberry strudel. Fixed price $29. ♕♕♕

★★½ **STELLA DEL MARE**—346 Lexington Avenue (at 40th Street)—687-4425—A warm, lovely, brick-walled Italian restaurant with few pretensions and solid, good cooking. Owner Joe Lucin sees to every detail. Skip the antipasti and go for the gnocchi with asparagus, the whole snapper in garlic and oil, and the butterflied lamb. Avoid the smoky downstairs piano bar. $$$$ ♕♕

★★½ **DOCK'S**—633 Third Avenue (near 40th Street)—986-8080—An East Side branch of a West Side original, this is an honest seafood house with a good selection, a pleasant atmosphere of white tiles and big central bar, but you can't help feeling you're in a concept restaurant in Atlanta. Good clam chowder, grilled fish. $$$$ ♕♕

♡ ★★★★ **GRAND CENTRAL OYSTER BAR & RESTAURANT**—Grand Central Terminal—490-6650—Opened in 1912, this granddaddy of American seafood restaurants is renowned for its extraordinary offerings of oysters and every kind of fish that swims into the Fulton Market. An astounding space to eat in (underneath the Terminal's Great Hall), it is always crowded at lunch (less so at dinner) and there's a quieter rear room/bar, as well as counters and that famous oyster bar. Don't try coming late for your reservation or you'll lose it. The range of offerings here is the best you'll ever see and it's all prepared with great integrity. The wine list is very long in American whites. Chowders, grilled fish, smoked salmon. Closed Sat. & Sun. $$$$ ♕♕♕♕

★★ **EXTRA! EXTRA!**—767 Second Avenue (in the Daily News Building at 42nd Street)—490-2900—Yes, it really is black and white and red all over, with eclectic offerings from the kitchen such as Indian onion fritters with banana-tamarind chutney, the

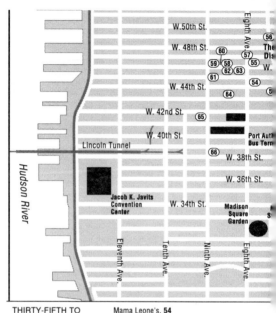

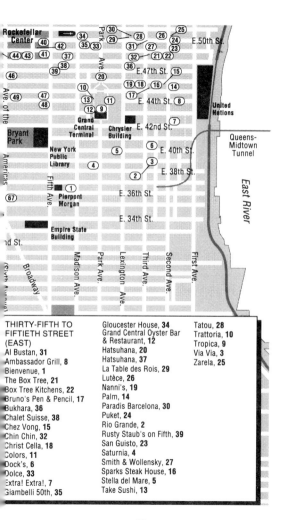

Rockefeller Center

E. 50th St.

Park Ave.

E. 47th St.

E. 44th St.

Grand Central Terminal

Chrysler Building

E. 42nd St.

Bryant Park

New York Public Library

E. 40th St.

United Nations

Queens-Midtown Tunnel

Americas

E. 38th St.

Fifth Ave.

Pierpont Morgan

E. 36th St.

East River

Empire State Building

E. 34th St.

3d St.

Madison Ave.

Park Ave.

Lexington Ave.

Third Ave.

Second Ave.

First Ave.

Broadway

Sixth Avenue

Ave. of the

THIRTY-FIFTH TO FIFTIETH STREET (EAST)
Al Bustan, **31**
Ambassador Grill, **8**
Bienvenue, **1**
The Box Tree, **21**
Box Tree Kitchens, **26**
Bruno's Pen & Pencil, **17**
Bukhara, **36**
Chalet Suisse, **38**
Chez Vong, **15**
Chin Chin, **32**
Christ Cella, **18**
Colors, **11**
Dock's, **6**
Dolce, **33**
Extra! Extra!, **7**
Giambelli 50th, **35**

Gloucester House, **34**
Grand Central Oyster Bar & Restaurant, **12**
Hatsuhana, **20**
Hatsuhana, **37**
La Table des Rois, **29**
Lutèce, **26**
Nanni's, **19**
Palm, **14**
Paradis Barcelona, **30**
Puket, **24**
Rio Grande, **2**
Rusty Staub's on Fifth, **39**
San Guisto, **23**
Saturnia, **4**
Smith & Wollensky, **27**
Sparks Steak House, **16**
Stella del Mare, **5**
Take Sushi, **13**

Tatou, **28**
Trattoria, **10**
Tropica, **9**
Via Via, **3**
Zarela, **25**

Dagwood Sandwich With Everything, (breast of chicken, ham, salami, cheese, etc.) and fried calamari with chipolte sauce. A friendly and lively spot for lunch in particular. Closed Sunday. $$½ ♟

★★★★ **AMBASSADOR GRILL**—1 UN Plaza (near First Avenue in the UN Plaza Hotel)—702-5014—More than just another hotel restaurant, the Ambassador Grill attracts a mixed crowd of area residents and resident aliens (from the adjacent UN complex). An attractive modern decor replete with a mirrored greenhouse ceiling and inlaid marble floor is the setting for chef Walter Houlihan's eclectic contemporary cuisine. Gorgonzola and wild mushroom tartlet, smoked salmon on a potato buckwheat pancake with asparagus, roasted monkfish with tortilla crust, spicy grilled chicken with tomatillo salsa, chocolate raspberry creamcake, ice cream and apricot quenelles in a tuile crust with fruit coulis. International wine list. $$$ ♟♟♟

★★½ **TROPICA**—Pan Am Building Concourse (above Grand Central Terminal)—867-6767—What a charming and quite unexpected place this is! If it were in Atlanta or Tampa or even Houston, it would be one of the best spots in town. In New York it doesn't rank that high, but what it does, it does quite nicely, starting with a happy greeting, a winsome, slightly Caribbean-plantation house look, an open kitchen and a pleasant bar (complete with monitors to tell commuters when the next train leaves). The mostly seafood menu has some real zest to it, and this is a great spot for lunch. Crab cakes with field greens and mustard sauce, conch chowder with okra, tamarind BBQ shrimp. Closed Saturday. $$$ ♟

★ **TRATTORIA**—200 Park Avenue (at 44th Street)—661-3090—A sprawling, enjoyable spot for lunch. The portions are large but the pasta generally overcooked and served with a certain lack of grace by the waiters, most of whom wish they were working in a posher place. The once-stellar gelati is now mundane. $$$ ♟♟

★½ **COLORS**—237 Park Avenue (at 44th Street)—661-2000—Racing colors give this glossy dining room

40

its name, and the bar crowd seems to enjoy itself thoroughly, as you'll amply hear from your table in the dining room. The food is basically Italian, with nothing all that good but nothing all that poor either. "O.K." seems to be the operative word here in dishes like sautéed mushrooms, penne all'amatriciana, and sausages and peppers. Closed Saturday & Sunday. $$$½ ♀

★★ **TAKE-SUSHI**—71 Vanderbilt Avenue (near 44th Street)—867-5120—Fast-paced and entirely worthwhile Japanese spot for excellent sushi at the bar. Won't cost much and you'll have a good time. Closed Sunday. $$ ♀

★★★½ **PALM**—837 Second Avenue (at 45th Street)—687-2953—Since the 1920s Palm has been the great New York steakhouse par excellence—though hardly for its decor. There's sawdust on the floor, discolored murals of favorite customers, a much-too-smoky, cramped bar where you'll probably wait any time after 6 PM, and waiters who don't hold much truck with the amenities. You come here for 16-ounce aged steaks, gargantuan lobsters, great cheesecake and anything else on the menu (well, the spaghetti's not so good). The wine list is a joke. Palm Too is located right across the street and is just as good though not as antique. $$$$½ ♀

★★★ **BRUNO'S PEN & PENCIL**—205 East 45th Street (near Third Avenue)— 682-8660—If you want to get a feel for New York in the 1940s and 1950s, when journalists and artists regaled themselves in oaky bars on generous drinks and great steaks, Pen & Pencil is for you. The place is a throwback— dark woods, sporting paraphernalia, comfy banquettes, waiters in white jackets. The red meats are among the very best in the city—you just won't find better lamb chops or prime rib anywhere. Appetizers are not. The wine list needs some updating too. $$$$½ ♀♀

★★★★ **HATSUHANA**—237 Park Avenue (on 46th St)—661-3400—and 17 East 48th Street (near Madison Avenue)—355-3345—Long considered NYC's best sushi restaurant, with two locations. The original, 48th Street restaurant is pleasant enough, while the newer, Park Avenue branch (actually wedged off the Avenue between the streets) is prettier, with a greenhouse dining room. At both places you'll find Japanese businessmen at the sushi bar or tables challenging the itamae chef to come up with something interesting. He always does—from mackerel and pickled ginger to broiled squid feet. For those with more conservative tastes, you can count on excellent tempura, sashimi, tekka maki, salmon teriyaki. $$$$½ ♀

★★ **NANNI'S**—146 East 46th Street (near Lexington Avenue)—599-9684—A barren, pushy, cramped Italian restaurant serving very good pastas and mediocre entrees at exorbitant prices. Wine list is no credit either. Cappelletti alla Nanni. $$$$ ♀♀

★★ **CHRIST CELLA**—160 East 46th Street (near Lexington Avenue)—697-2479—What brings the heavy-hitting-expense-account crowd here is beyond us: the US Prime steaks and fresh seafood are unassailably of high quality but it's all priced above its close competitors' like Palm, Sparks and Smith & Wollensky, and it's all served by a smug staff with the subtlety of a construction foreman. Regulars may get slightly better treatment, but don't you count on it. The premises were never particularly inviting, but the beefeaters who come here seem to love it that way. You can forget the wine list. $$$$$ ♀

★★★★ **SPARKS STEAK HOUSE**—210 East 46th Street (near Third Avenue)—687-4855—Paradise for the oenophile or even the amateur wine buff curious about sampling mature vintages of French, California, Italian, or Spanish wine. The indefatigable owner, Pat Cetta, is forever updating his cellar, and lays claim to one of the biggest collections of fine and rare wine in the city. What's more, his mark-ups are reasonable. Opt for Sparks signature steak au fromage and inquire about the reserve cabernet sauvignons he may have in stock. (In fairness, beef is hardly de rigueur; you can choose from a wide array of seafood, fowl, lamb and veal dishes.) And how about capping off the evening with cheesecake and a late harvest riesling or a Sauternes? Sublime! $$$$½ 🍷🍷🍷🍷

★★½ **CHEZ VONG**—220 East 46th Street (between Second and Third Avenues)—867-1111—Very deluxe, very expensive Paris transplant serving Cantonese and Szechwan cuisines. The interior is chock full of antiques. Dumplings, dim sum, jelly fish salad, beggar chicken, Peking duck. Good wine list and amiable service. $$$ 🍷

★★½ **RUSTY STAUB'S ON FIFTH**—575 Fifth Avenue (at 47th Street)—682-1000—Former baseball player Rusty Staub's restaurant boasts a menu worthy of a Met: steaks, chops, burgers and the like. But more challenging entries like grilled mahi mahi with black bean sauce, and seared salmon filet with scallion cake also appear, and the wine list (Staub's introduction to oenophilia came first-hand from Seagram's Charles Bronfman who also happened to own the Montreal Expos during Staub's stint there) is spectacular. $$$ 🍷🍷🍷

★★ **CHALET SUISSE**—6 East 48th Street (near Fifth Avenue)—355-0855—In both food and decor this place lives up to its name, and it's a pleasant diversion for lunch or before theater. The Swiss specialties are dependably good, and service is friendly. The fondue is excellent. $$$ 🍷🍷

★★★ **BUKHARA**—148 East 48th Street (between Lexington and Third Avenues)—838-1811—Bukhara stands out for specializing in the cooking of Uzbekistan, especially the wonderfully savory barbecued meats and luscious tandoori specials. You eat this food with your fingers amidst a sedate dining room full of glistening copper and Bukhara rugs. The prices are fair, the service courteous, and there's a good Sunday brunch too. Pork spareribs, Seekh kebab, Sikandari raan. $$$½ 🍷

★★ **DOLCE**—60 East 49th Street (between Park and Madison Avenues)—692-9292— If you like Sfuzzi (q.v.) you'll love this. The former site of Aurora, now with a colorized Milton Glazer interior and a less spacious, but leather-intensive seating scheme, has been taken over by a team with strong ties to Sfuzzi, the Dallas-based restaurant chain specializing in moderately priced Italian fare with a California accent. Grilled eggplant torta, myriad pizzas, Caesar salad, sausage stromboli, veal Dolce with chardonnay caper sauce. Good for a quick business lunch or a pre-theater dinner. $$½ ☷☷

★★★★ **SMITH & WOLLENSKY**—201 East 49th Street (on Third Avenue)—753-1530—A very large, handsome, oak-floored steak-and-seafood house that is clearly a mid-town institution. The steaks, veal chops, lobsters, and seafood are all top quality, and the wine list is quite extraordinary, especially in vintage claret and cabernet sauvignon. (Owner Alan Stillman boasts a 511 entry wine list and a 50,000 bottle cellar.) Service is brisk but adequate to the job, and this place is jammed with businessmen day and night, as is the more casual grill to the rear. Thanks to late night hours, it also attracts an after-theater crowd. Outdoor dining in the summer. A very New York "joint." $$$$½ ☷☷☷☷

★★★ **CHIN CHIN**—216 East 49th Street (near Third Avenue)—888-4555—Vintage photographs snapped in the Far East at the turn of the century, juxtaposed with bleached walls, plush banquettes, and dramatic lighting create a sleek, stark look. But because of its proximity to midtown offices, the atmosphere at Chin Chin after work can be boisterous. Nevertheless, the kitchen's output compensates for the din. Mixed dumplings, scallion pancake, lobster roll, spring roll, chicken Tung, glazed shrimp Grand Marnier, orange beef, fried rice. $$$½ ☷☷☷

★½ **BOX TREE KITCHENS**—252 East 49th Street (near Second Avenue)—758-8320—An appendage of proprietor Augustin Paege's more formal establishment next door, the Kitchen serves up less expensive and less elaborate fare than The Box Tree proper in a fanciful setting that could be described as Adirondack Art Nouveau. A limited menu includes grilled wild mushrooms, Caesar salad, Box Tree chicken club, wood-seared, herb-smoked, black angus rib-eye. Lunch only. $$$ ♟

★★★ **THE BOX TREE**—250 East 49th Street (near Second Avenue)—758-8320—A much touted "gem of a restaurant" with an intimate interior which verges on precious. Service, on the other hand, can be distinctly chilly. Yet the kitchen's creations—gratin of snails, haddock mousse, poached trout, fricassee of lobster, calf's liver with truffles, crème brûlée, and poached pears are quite admirable both in form and content. Sample them at lunch for $37.00 prix fixe, or at dinner, with the addition of such soups as lobster bisque, or salad with stilton for $76.00. Nice wine list. Amex only. ♟♟♟

★★ **SAN GIUSTO**—935 Second Avenue (near 49th Street)—319-0900—A hospitable dining room, popular with a business crowd at lunch. (Avoid the back annex). You can depend on traditional Italian stand-by's like roasted peppers and spaghetti carbonara. Ambitious specials like chicken stuffed with white truffles and porcini mushrooms don't always dazzle, so stick with the regular menu. $$$½ ♟♟

★★★ **GLOUCESTER HOUSE**—37 East 50th Street (near Madison Avenue)—838-7275—A great classic seafood house going back to the 1930s under Edmund Lillys' gentlemanly ownership. It's had its ups and downs over the decades, and was drifting into complacency for a while. The economy notwithstanding, things are on the upswing here, and the food is impeccably prepared—from the shortbread biscuits and fried onion rings to the beautifully cooked lobsters and seafood. The premises have an evocative decor you might associate with New England, with a slightly masculine feel. Salmon patties with béarnaise sauce, crab cakes, all lobster dishes, floating island, chocolate mousse. $$$$½ ♟♟♟

★★½ **GIAMBELLI 50TH**—46 East 50th Street (near Madison Avenue)—688-2760—Owner Adi Giovanetti has brought this spot back to life after years of coasting. It still does not have the snap of his other places, Il Nido, nor the luxury of his third, Il Monello, but the food is quite close. Prices are still very high, so order carefully, and split pastas. Gorgonzola ravioli, lobster ravioli, veal medallions in red wine sauce. $$$$½ ♙♙♙

★★½ **LA TABLE DES ROIS**—135 East 50th Street (near Third Avenue)—838-7275—A pleasant, unpretentious and satisfying alternative to many midtown eateries, nicely suited to a business lunch or a pre-theater dinner (the latter is available at a fixed price of $20.50). You can count on well executed bistro fare—salade aux lardons, soup à l'oignon, pâtés and terrines, leeks wrapped in prosciutto, grilled scallops, poached salmon, roasted veal. $$$ ♙♙

★½ **PARADIS BARCELONA**—145 East 50th Street (near Lexington Avenue)—754-3333—Despite its grand beauty and undeniable Spanish charm, this branch of a well-known Barcelona restaurant chain just hasn't come up to expectations. The food sounds wonderful but there's very little flavor in most dishes, and some are trite and boring. Service ranges from the nearly non-existent upwards to terrible. Good Spanish wine list. $$$$½ ♙♙♙

★★ **TATOU**—151 East 50th Street (near Third Avenue)—753-1144—Modeled on an old Opera House from the Deep South, Tatou attracts quite a cast of characters. This vast space is probably best suited for the office Christmas party or a gathering of out-of-towners. Yet the food is better than one might expect and portions are ample. Staff could be better trained. Creole pizza, crab cakes, spicy tomato soup, grilled Cornish hen, sea scallops with grapefruit and cilantro, veal chop, mocha crunch ice cream pie. Downstairs you dine to the accompaniment of live music. Upstairs, there's a popular nightclub—accessible by invitation only. $$$ ♙♙

★★★ **AL BUSTAN**—827 Third Avenue (near 50th Street)—759-5933—Located on the site that for years housed Le Bistro (with many of the former establishment's affable waiters still in place), Al Bustan lives up to its promise of providing fine Lebanese cuisine in a cheery, relaxed setting. Appetizers are so appealing that you might consider organizing a full meal around the likes of hummus bilahmeh (with minced meat and pignoli nuts) falafel, makanek (lamb sausage), baba ghanouj, and hindbeh bilzeit (simmered dandelion). Main courses and heavily scented desserts are less enticing. $$$½ 🍷

★★★★★ **LUTÈCE**—249 East 50th Street (near Second Avenue)—752-2225—Lutèce is widely regarded as the finest French restaurant in NYC—if not the country—a reputation based on chef/owner André Soltner's 30 years' worth of brilliant and dedicated service. The sprightly interior attracts a crowd of regulars who know they'll find perfection in every bite, plus a bevy of curious newcomers bent on discovering what the fuss is all about. Soltner plays no favorites, and will gladly choose the meal for either category of client—an experience well worth it. His extraordinary repertoire ranges from scallop beignets, home smoked roasted salmon, foie gras en brioche, baked lobster with shallots, red snapper goujonettes in red pepper sauce to roast guinea hen, caramelized rack of lamb, coffee praline Lutèce, cold chestnut soufflé. Extensive and expensive wine list. Monday dinner only. The fixed-price, $38 lunch is well worth it. Dinner is $60. 🍷🍷🍷🍷

★★ **PUKET**—945 Second Avenue (near 50th Street)—759-6339—A touch of Thailand tucked in midtown Manhattan, Puket has evolved a pleasing and authentic formula, but one which has become a tad routine over time. Friendly service and an inviting interior set the stage nonetheless. Fried wonton, prawns, all satés, sautéed beef with red pepper and onions, deep fried fish, fried rice noodle with chicken and crushed peanuts. Festive cocktails. $$$ 🍷

★★★½ **ZARELA**—953 Second Avenue (near 50th Street)—644-6740—Anyone in search of authentic Mexican cuisine served up in a cozy, fetching environment need go no further. Owner Zarela Martinez' trademark dishes include red snapper hash, chicken chilaquiles, squid veracruzana, salmon ahumado, and whole grilled trout, along with basics like melted cheese and chorizo, refried beans and fajitas. Sample the fried plantains, and try to leave room for the luscious desserts, especially the chocolate cake and the maple walnut pumpkin cheesecake. $$½ 🍷🍷

THIRTY-FIFTH TO
FIFTIETH STREET (WEST)

★★ **KEEN'S**—72 West 36th Street (near Avenue of the Americas)—947-3636—Old-time, refurbished and kept lively by a dedicated management, this place still has the clay pipes of its bygone customers racked on the ceiling, and the private dining rooms have an antique interest that makes this place almost as special as their famous mutton chops (rarely found anywhere else). The other food may be hit-or-miss. Nice wine list. $$$$½ 🍷🍷🍷

★ **MANGANARO**—488 Ninth Avenue (near 38th Street)—563-5331—The "restaurant" located at the back of this celebrated old world Italian charcuterie is worth the experience. Great meatballs, veal sausage, hero sandwiches. No credit cards. $ 🍷

★★ **CHEZ JOSEPHINE**—414 West 42nd Street (near Ninth Avenue)—594-1925—Quintessential French bistro fare—quail, roast chicken, frites—served in a setting designed as a homage to the late Josephine Baker (the owner is her adopted son). The place is decked out with paintings and posters from the period when Baker was all the rage in Paris. Even the famed piano on which she used to practice has been restored and is now occupied by a modern-day chanteuse who evokes a bygone era. Great fun. $$$ 🍷🍷

★★ **THE CENTURY CAFE**—132 West 43rd Street (near Avenue of the Americas)—398-1988—This is a sleek place that looks like an ocean liner, and the waitresses are waiting to be discovered by a Broadway agent. The food—seafood, salads, lighter fare—is OK, even if the kitchen tries to appeal to everyone's taste. $$½ 🍷🍷

● **THE NILE**—327 West 43rd Street (between Eighth and Ninth Avenues)—262-1111—If you are desperate to witness some authentic belly dancing and exotic entertainment, you might consider coming here for a drink and a nibble (the mezzei—felafal, hummus and tabbouleh are acceptable). Skip the full-course dinner, however, which is very poorly orchestrated, not that well-prepared and rather expensive. Regrettably, the Nile is more of a tourist trap than the entertaining excursion it could have been. Fixed price dinner $49. ▽

★½ **JEWEL OF INDIA**—15 West 44th Street (near Fifth Avenue)—869-5544—Despite an expensive face-lift, the Jewel of India fails to sparkle. You can expect standard Indian fare—assorted appetizers, lamb or prawns vindaloo, tandoori chicken, dal—served up at a snail's pace. $$$ ▽

★★ **CAFE 44**—44 West 44th Street (near Fifth Avenue in The Royalton Hotel)—869-4400—Without a doubt, this is one of the hippest, contemporary interiors in New York, designed by Philippe Stark. It opened with great fanfare, but after multiple changes of chefs, and subsequent problems in the kitchen, this remains a big question mark in terms of consistency. You can still expect an eclectic lunch or dinner, and the restaurant's proximity to Broadway makes it a convenient spot for a pre- or post-theater meal. The lounge is a must-see both for its decor and its glamorous clientele. $$$ ▽▽

★½ **THE ALGONQUIN**—59 West 44th Street (near Avenue of the Americas)—840-6800—In the main dining room, expect standard fare like lobster and lump crabmeat, supreme de volaille—and attentive service. The club-like lobby remains a popular spot for a drink. Unfortunately, in the cabaret, where New Yorkers and out-of-towners alike gather to hear first-rate musical performances, things have taken a turn for the worse. The menu is simplistic and hardly worthy of the entertainment. $$$½ ▽▽

● **UN DEUX TROIS**—123 West 44th Street (near 7th Ave.)—354-4148—There's a real spark of Times Square here, and the clientele is glitzy in the extreme. Would that the food—which is abysmal—matched the decor. The waiters are waiting for their big break in the theater; maybe they should try acting like waiters first. $$$ ▽

○ ★★ **SARDI'S**—234 West 44th Street (near Broadway)—221-8440—This legendary Broadway restaurant where opening nights are traditionally celebrated has been spruced up and is back in the hands of the ebullient Vincent Sardi, who still knows how to show a crowd a good time. The menu is as old fashioned as ever, but some of the entrées seem fresher than they used to. Go with the dishes "à la Sardi." Fixed price pre-theater dinner $34.95. $$$½ ♀

○ ★½ **MAMMA LEONE'S**—261 West 44th (near Eighth Avenue)—391-8270—The place retains the same hilarious, frenetic pace as always; the tour buses disgorge their customers, and the old-time waiters dash around with platters of antipasti and pasta, while magicians and clowns entertain the kids. Mamma Leone's has been trashed for its food over the years, but in fact, at these prices—$18.95–$29.95 for a full-course meal—it's amazing they do as decent a job as they do. The food is as good as you'll find in most out-of-town Italian restaurants around the USA, though in NYC that's not saying too much. Go with your family, have a good time, see a show, don't expect the culinary sublime. $$$ ♀♀

★★½ **CABANA CARIOCA**—123 West 45th Street (near Seventh Avenue)—581-8088—It may look dingy (you go up a flight of stairs to a thickly varnished, rather weird looking dining room; just follow the music), but Cabana Carioca serves the best Brazilian food in New York—great platters and pots steaming with black beans, manioc flour, feijoada (the Brazilian national stew), and seafood. All of it is lusty and filling and not particularly expensive. $$$ ♀

★★ **JEZEBEL**—630 Ninth Avenue (at 45th Street)—582-1045—Colorful and warmly decorated Soul food emporium way over West serving ribs, ham hocks, chicken, and sausages. Food is a little heavy for pre-theater consumption. $$ ♀

★★ **WOO LAE OAK OF SEOUL**—77 West 46th Street (near Avenue of the Americas)—869-9958—No one is raving about Korean cuisine in NYC, but this is a good place with a handsome atmosphere and pretty Oriental waitresses. The barbecue dishes, served on a grill on which you cook your own meat, are the best choices here. $$ ☖

★ **THE MEZZANINE**—235 West 46th Street (near Eighth Avenue in the Paramount Hotel)—764-5500—Welcome to the planet Uranus. You walk into a bizarre postmodern lobby, are greeted by automatons in oversized black suits, shown upstairs to the mezzanine restaurant and told they have no liquor license and that you can't even bring your own bottle of wine. Below you a group of seemingly anesthetized lounge lizards stare off into space while you try to find something from the California style menu you feel like eating—O.K. chili, O.K. onion soup, O.K. grilled chicken salad, dreadful pasta stuck to the plate, and yummy childish desserts. What a drag it is to be so hip! $$½

★★★★ **BARBETTA**—321 West 46th Street (near Eighth Avenue)—246-9171—This is NYC's oldest Italian restaurant and an elegant beauty run by Laura Maioglio. Every great musician and actor has eaten here, including Toscanini. The premises are set in a lovely townhouse, with a delightful garden for warm weather dining. Upstairs are elegant private dining rooms. The pre-theater crowd is a bit rushed here, but you won't find better food in the neighborhood. Linguine with black olive paste, sensational risotto with rosé Champagne, sturgeon with olives and fennel. There is a pre-theater menu priced at $39 and a seven-course tasting menu at $55. A la carte. $$$$$ ☖☖☖

★★★½ **ORSO**—322 West 46th Street (near Eighth Avenue)—489-7212—By far the most popular restaurant in the Theater District. It's even tough to get a table after theater. The reasons are not far to seek: the atmosphere is unpretentious, the greeting at the door warm (and apologetic if they can't fit you in), the price is very reasonable, and the rustic trattoria fare is very good indeed. It gets its fair share of celebrities too. Ravioli with potato and sage butter, grilled chicken with beans and garlic, polenta with cheese and lentils. Good pizzas at $8.50. $$$½ ☖☖

★★ **JOE ALLEN**—326 West 46th Street (near Eighth

Avenue)—581-6464—A long-time hangout for theater-goers and actors, Joe Allen (there's an L.A. branch) has no pretensions and pretty decent, simple food. The ribs and burgers are dependable, the service affable (often by actors between jobs), and the place buzzes with a certain theatrical history. It's a good spot before or after the show. MC and Visa only. $$$ ♀

★★★ **CAROLINA**—355 West 46th Street (between Eighth and Ninth Avenues)—245-0058—Carolina has returned to its Southwest origins after a brief stint serving provençal fare on the same premises under the name Café Cassis. Gone are the pizzette and frisé. Back are barbecued ribs, chili, Texas skirt steak, grilled hot smoked sausages with home-made mustard, crab cakes Maryland and smoky shrimp over linguine with salsa. Like many a Broadway revival, this popular pre- and after-theater spot with a cheery bar room and mirrored dining area in back, is an instant hit. $$$ ♀♀

★★½ **LATTANZI**—361 West 46th Street (near Ninth Avenue)—315-0980—Despite its insipid decor and cramped quarters, a service staff that seems always distracted, and one of NYC's most absurdly priced and dull wine lists, when Lattanzi does get the food out of the kitchen it can be delicious and full flavored. The place is jammed pre-theater, so book after 8 PM, when a second menu featuring dishes favored by Rome's Italian-Jewish community is proffered and the staff not quite so harried. Artichokes alla Giudea, ravioli with porcinis, fettuccine with stracotto beef, snapper with raisins and vinegar. $$$½ ♀

★★★½ **ZEN PALATE**—663 Ninth Avenue (entrance on 46th Street)—582-1669—Here's a real find: don't be put off by the name, the fact that this is a vegetarian restaurant or the silly philosophic menu lingo. Not only is it a smart-looking place with ochre walls, cloud-painted ceiling, and wicker café chairs, but the food is sensational. And because there are a number of fried items here, you get enough fat in your meal to satisfy your appetite and you definitely won't leave hungry. You can even skip the rather insipid desserts. Moo-shu basil rolls, "Dream Land" spinach linguine, steamed dumplings. At press-time, Zen Palate is still B.Y.O.B. $$½

★★ **B. SMITH'S**—771 Eighth Avenue (at 47th Street)—247-2222—A large, sleek, dramatic space, convenient to the theater district. The menu is eclectic and suits any dining mood. Grilled smoked mozzarella with tomatoes and peppers, grilled wild mushrooms, veal scaloppini, pork chop, shrimp scampi with fried plantains, and coconut tuile with white chocolate ice cream. A selection of "Light Plates" is available for after theater nibbling. $$$ ⚲

★ **CHARLEY O'S**—33 West 48th Street (near Fifth Avenue)—582-7141—Really a restaurant attached to a very active saloon, but the steaks, chops, sandwiches and corned beef hash are fine enough, and the drinks are generous. $$$ ⚲

★★ **RAGA**—57 West 48th Street (near Avenue of the Americas)—757-3450—This sensuous restaurant showed that Indian dining rooms can be every bit as elegant and refined as French or Italian restaurants. From the ornate door to the seductive lighting, this is a beautifully designed room, but the service staff can ruin a meal here. Some of the food can be first-rate, like the vindaloo dishes, but much of it has become lackluster in recent years. The breads are still wonderful. $$$$ ⚲

★★ **BROADWAY GRILL**—1605 Broadway (near 49th Street in the Holiday Inn Crowne Plaza Hotel)—315-6161—There has been a concerted effort to make this restaurant more than another obligatory hotel appendage. An ambitious menu devised by David Liederman, formerly of Chez Louis: soft shell crabs with black bean sauce, grilled poussin, wild mushroom pizza, upside-down cake. However, on separate visits our meals came up short on flavor. $$$ ⚲⚲

★★★★ **LA RESERVE**—4 West 49th Street (near Fifth Avenue)—247-2993—Catty-corner to Rockefeller Center is this airy, stylish restaurant with two handsomely decorated dining areas and a commodious private dining room downstairs. Owner Jean-Louis Missud is one of New York's most genteel hosts and his chef, Dominique Payraudeau, carries on the tradition here of imaginative modern French cuisine without ever going overboard. Sea bass with black truffles, poached salmon with lentils, stuffed loin of veal, lemon-lime cake, apple tart. $49 fixed price ($40 pre-theatre dinner). ♥♥♥

○ ★★★½ **THE RAINBOW ROOM**—30 Rockefeller Plaza (near 49th Street)—632-5000—Towering over mid-town Manhattan, this is still one of the most dramatic settings on the Manhattan restaurant circuit. Restaurateurs Joe Baum and Michael Whiteman, together with architect Hugh Hardy, marshaled $25 million to renovate and revitalize one of the city's greatest institutions. An initial effort to offer bygone classics like tournedos rossini and baked Alaska alongside contemporary dishes was abandoned in favor of a more standard modern menu that lacked character. But at press time, a new chef has come aboard, so stay tuned. An extensive but expensive wine list, full of vintage treasures. The musical entertainment changes regularly. So go with a group, dress festively, and don't forget your dancing shoes. By day, The Rainbow Room functions as a private club. Closed Monday. Amex only. $$$$$ ♥♥♥♥

★★ **SEA GRILL**—19 West 49th Street (at Rockefeller Center)—246-9201—Only the service has improved at the Sea Grill since our last report, and the hiring of the former chef of the Four Seasons, Seppi Renggli, hasn't done much to bring the menu here into any kind of enticing focus. The standard seafood dishes are all right, more creative ones good, but at the prices charged here, you're probably paying more for the glorious view of the skating rink and skyscrapers than for the high quality of the cuisine. $$$$$ ♥♥♥

○ ★★ **AMERICAN FESTIVAL CAFE**—20 West 50th Street (in Rockefeller Center)—246-6699—If you have time for just one stop for a family outing in NYC, this should be it. Set right on Rockefeller Center skating rink under the gaze of Prometheus and the umbrella of skyscrapers, the dining room is decorated with fine folk art in a casual, amiable way. The food sticks to American classics with a few nice modern touches, but prices have gotten quite high and the quality of food seems to have slipped somewhat. Nevertheless great for Christmas time under that famous tree. Service can be lax. Prime rib, crabcakes with cole slaw. $$$ 🍷🍷

FIFTY-FIRST TO
SIXTY-FIFTH STREET (EAST)

★★½ **SHINWA**—645 Fifth Avenue (entrance on 51st Street between Madison and Fifth Avenues in the Olympic Towers)—644-7400—Judging by the crowd of regulars, this is one of midtown's more authentic Japanese eateries. There are several dining rooms from which to choose, and the most popular seems to be the one with a courtyard view. Very filling soups including niku (sliced beef) and kamo (sliced duck), kaiso salad and kou no mono (homemade pickles). Specialties include unagi kabayaki (broiled eel) and udon suki (noodles, vegetables and seafood simmered in a fish broth), plus traditional tempura, sashimi and wafu steak. Kaiseki meals available for $38. $$$$ 🍷

★★ **TSE YANG**—34 East 51st Street (near Madison Avenue)—688-5447—It's a pity that the food does not live up to the elegance of the decor, for this is surely an attractive place to dine, like its twin in Paris. Standard fare such as spring and autumn rolls, lemon sweet and sour pork, and lobster Szechuan are ultra-expensive. $$$$ 🍷🍷

★★★½ **LA GRENOUILLE**—3 East 52nd Street (near Fifth Avenue)—752-1495—La Grenouille may still be the most beautiful and romantic restaurant in NYC—certainly the most divine floral arrangements in town—and we applaud the Masson family's dedication to classic French cuisine for more than a quarter century. Yet their classicism seems so prescribed and simplistic that it's hard to get excited about a menu that rarely changes and that offers so little in the way of specials. We can appreciate the textbook perfection of a Potage St. Germain, asparagus in puff pastry, Dover sole, pot au feu, and Grand Marnier souffle found night after night, but one cannot dismiss lightly

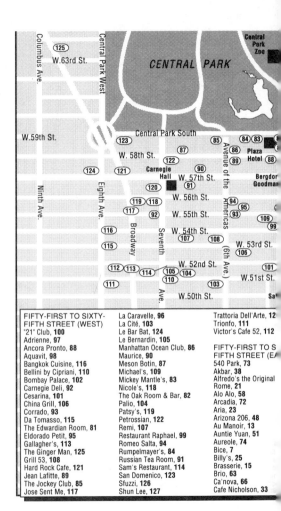

Columbus Ave.
Central Park West
W.63rd St.
(125)

CENTRAL PARK

Central Park Zoo

W.59th St.

Central Park South
(123)

W. 58th St.
(122)

Avenue of the Americas

Plaza Hotel
(84)(83)
(85)
(87)
(86)
(89)(88)

Carnegie Hall
(124)(121)
(120)
W. 57th St.
(90)
(91)

Bergdorf Goodman

Ninth Ave.
Eighth Ave.

W. 56th St.
(119)(118)
(117)
(92)

W. 55th St.
(116)
(94)
(95)
(93)
(109)
(99)

Broadway
Seventh Ave.

W. 54th St.
(115)
(107)
(108)

W. 53rd St.
(106)

W. 52nd St.
(112)(113)
(114)
(105)(104)
(110)
(101)

W.51st St.
(111)
(103)

(6th Ave.)

W.50th St.

Sa

56

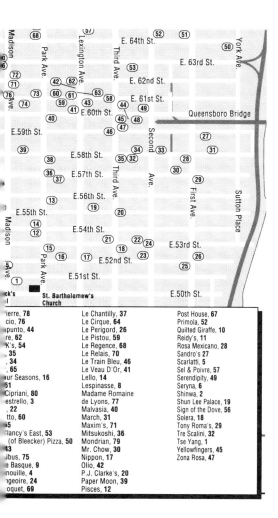

ierre, **78**
cio, **76**
punto, **44**
re, **62**
K's, **54**
, **35**
, **34**
, **65**
ur Seasons, **16**
61
Cipriani, **80**
estrello, **3**
, **22**
tto, **60**
5
lancy's East, **53**
(of Bleecker) Pizza, **50**
43
ibus, **75**
e Basque, **9**
nouille, **4**
geoire, **24**
oquet, **69**

Le Chantilly, **37**
Le Cirque, **64**
Le Perigord, **26**
Le Pistou, **59**
Le Regence, **68**
Le Relais, **70**
Le Train Bleu, **46**
Le Veau D'Or, **41**
Lello, **14**
Lespinasse, **8**
Madame Romaine
de Lyons, **77**
Malvasia, **40**
March, **31**
Maxim's, **71**
Mitsukoshi, **36**
Mondrian, **79**
Mr. Chow, **30**
Nippon, **17**
Olio, **42**
P.J. Clarke's, **20**
Paper Moon, **39**
Pisces, **12**

Post House, **67**
Primola, **52**
Quilted Giraffe, **10**
Reidy's, **11**
Rosa Mexicano, **28**
Sandro's **27**
Scarlatti, **5**
Sel & Poivre, **57**
Serendipity, **49**
Seryna, **6**
Shinwa, **2**
Shun Lee Palace, **19**
Sign of the Dove, **56**
Solera, **18**
Tony Roma's, **29**
Tre Scalini, **32**
Tse Yang, **1**
Yellowfingers, **45**
Zona Rosa, **47**

La Grenouille's refusal to evolve in step with modern times. Excellent but very pricey wine list. Fixed price $68. ♥♥♥♥

★★ ½ **IL MENESTRELLO**—14 East 52nd Street (near Fifth Avenue)—421-7588—Fifteen years has not dimmed the bright allure of Il Menestrello, which has consistently turned out fine Northern Italian food with gracious savoire faire under Milan Miletic. The two-story restaurant is peach-colored with dramatic art. The only problem is that Il Menestrello's pasta dishes are so high priced at a time when other restaurants are reducing the tab for that course. Pappardelle with mushrooms, sautéed fresh shrimp, stuffed veal chop, fruit desserts. $$$$½ ♥♥

★★★★ **SCARLATTI**—34 East 52nd Street (near Madison Avenue)—753-2444—Despite the current recession, owner Lello Arpaia maintains this elegant dining room with savoir-faire and a menu of classic and modern Italian specialties, the best of which have a Southern twist. The staff can sometimes be too mannered ("Let me suggest a nice veal chop for the young lady"), but Lello is a dedicated restaurateur who really wants you to have a great meal. Malfatti pasta with artichokes, calamari freddo, sea bass with herbs, ravioli with cream and saffron, penne with smoked cheese and fresh tomato, viti with veal ragu, risotto al frutti di mare, snapper with olive oil. $$$$½ ♥♥♥♥

○ ★★★★★ **THE FOUR SEASONS**—99 East 52nd Street (near Park Avenue)—754-9494—One of NYC's most important and beautiful restaurants. Its location in the Mies Van der Rohe-designed Seagram Building and its Philip Johnson interior have given it unique landmark status, and indefatigable owners Tom Margittai and Paul Kovi, together with managers Julian Niccolini and Alex von Bidder, run the handsome Grill Room for the delectation of those who created the Power Lunch concept. The Pool Room is more romantic, especially for dinner. The food is of very high quality, though no longer the trailblazing cuisine of the past. Crisped shrimp in fruit and mustard sauce, tuna carpaccio, frogs' legs curry, fresh venison or pheasant, loin of rabbit with polenta, rack of lamb, chocolate velvet cake, or the highly popular spa cuisine. Prices are very high, but the $41.50 Grill Room dinner menu is an outright steal. The wine list is stellar, the service reserved, but most professional. $$$$$ ♛♛♛♛

★★★½ **NIPPON**—155 East 52nd Street (near Lexington Avenue)—688-5941—One of the first modern Japanese restaurants in the United States, Nippon has long been a pioneer in everything from fine decor and tatami rooms to bringing sushi and sashimi to the attention of the American public. This is where the negimaki roll was created, to satisfy Americans' taste for beef with a Japanese counterpoint. The restaurant is large and bright and the staff is very cordial to everyone who comes here. The best idea is to allow the chef to prepare a special dinner for you featuring everything from imaginative sushi to exotic main courses. The tatami rooms are for parties, and the meal will be unforgettable. $$$½ ♛

★★★ **ARIA**—253 East 52nd Street (near Second Avenue)—888-1410—Anyone who hasn't visited this spot since Aria replaced the rather staid Café Argenteuil is in for a pleasant surprise: it is now a very inviting, fresh-looking dining room. As the name Aria suggests, you dine to the accompaniment of softly piped in classical music. But the menu is as contemporary as the decor—asparagus with roast pepper vinaigrette, Caesar salad with polenta croutons, cavatelli pomodoro, yellowfin tuna with sun-dried tomatoes, grilled swordfish, sautéed free range chicken with luganica sausage. $$$ ♛♛

★★ **BILLY'S**—948 First Avenue (near 52nd Street)—355-8920—A fair price for a fair meal. This neighborhood pub has been serving up seafood, steaks, chops, burgers and corn beef hash—a house specialty—for the better part of the century, and numbers many a devoted regular. The Olde New York decor is completely apt for a pleasant lunch or early dinner. $$ ♛

★★★★★ **LE PERIGORD**—405 East 52nd Street (near First Avenue)—755-6244—This deluxe French restaurant is a perfect example of how classicism and modernity can coexist with great success, year after year. Under owner Georges Briguet, this has long been one of Manhattan's most elegant dining rooms, and, under chef Antoine Bouterin, the kitchen is truly inspired. Soft lighting, pretty flowered accents and a respectful staff make this a very romantic place, and no one is better than Briguet in making a newcomer feel right at home. Put yourself in Bouterin's hands or go with his specials. Wine prices from a superb list are quite reasonable. Smoked salmon tart, red snapper in red wine and pepper sauce, quail with julienne of vegetables, beef with truffles on a potato galette, halibut in bouillon, tuna steak with anchovy butter, gratin of raspberries, passion fruit mousse, caramelized pear sandwich. Fixed price dinner $49 a bargain. $$$$½ 🍷🍷🍷🍷

★★ **SERYNA**—11 East 53rd Street (near Madison Avenue)—980-9393—Exotic Japanese interior with an enterprising menu featuring prime beef cooked on a sizzling stone as well as traditional sushi, sashimi and tempura dishes. Beware lunch-time minimums that presuppose expense-account dining. $$$$$ 🍷🍷

★★ **BRASSERIE**—100 East 53rd Street (near Park Ave)—751-4840—At any hour of the day or night—24 hours a day, that is—you can find something good to eat at the Brasserie, which can come in handy after a full night at the opera or a brisk early morning walk. The subterranean dining room is bright, cheerful and serves a good rendering of French bistro classics—the heartier the better. There's a rectangular counter where you may sit for a quick or solitary meal. $$$ 🍷

★★★ **ALFREDO'S THE ORIGINAL OF ROME**—153 East 53rd Street (near Third Avenue in the Citicorp Building)—371-3367—Despite the hoopla about its links to the glamorous Alfredo's of Rome and its tucked-away location, this popular spot also happens to serve Italian food of a very, very high order. Owner Guido Bellanca and his sons work hard to maintain a high level of cooking, as do the chefs regularly brought in from Italy, and you won't go wrong with any of the pastas, especially the famous fettuccine al'Alfredo, the risotto with mascarpone and spinach, or the panzotti with walnuts and herbs. Also recommended are the tiramisu and gelati. $$$½ ♀

★★★ **SOLERA**—216 East 53rd Street (near Lexington Avenue)—644-1166—The brightest and most convivial of Spanish restaurants to open in New York recently, Solera demonstrates just how savory modern Spanish cuisine and wine can be. The chef and co-owner, Dominic Cerrone, trained at Le Bernardin, and it shows in his seafood dishes like monkfish in cream and tomato and grilled shrimp in herbs. Superb vegetable paella, gazpacho, roasted duck with sherry and green olives, crema catalana—all at quite moderate prices. The wine list is full of the best Spain has to offer. $$$½ ♀♀♀

★★★★½ **IL NIDO**—251 East 53rd Street (near Second Avenue)—753-8450—This is a bastion for Northern Italian (specifically, Tuscan) cuisine, and it caters to a clientele who are prepared to pay a hefty tab for some of the best food in New York. The dining room is sophisticated without being studied—dark wood beams, white walls, plaid carpet and a sea of white tablecloths. Ask owner Adi Giovanetti what he'd suggest for an evening and you'll be very happy you did. Ravioli with truffles, Tuscan chicken with pignoli and mint, venison in red wine, farfalle with duck ragu, tiramisu, raspberries with warm zabaglione. The wine list is full of classic and contemporary entries. $$$$$ ♀♀♀♀

★★½ **LA MANGEOIRE**—1008 Second Avenue (at 53rd Street)—759-7086—This midtown French bistro has for years been a popular spot for a business lunch or casual dinner. A faint and somewhat bygone evocation of the south of France, the comforting interior is nonetheless very pleasant. Eggplant and goat cheese terrine, seafood ravioli. $$$ ♀♀

★★½ **BICE**—7 East 54th Street (near Fifth Avenue)—688-1999—Still immensely popular with the fashion trade and trend setters who made it a destination restaurant, Bice shows no sign of receding. Indeed, the lunch-hour din recalls a sporting event at Shea Stadium. However, frequent chef changes make this a problemmatic restaurant to recommend for the food, and service seems to depend on the whim of the evening. Bresaola with artichokes, crostino di mozzarella e pomodoro, maccheroni with sausage and fennel, lobster ravioli with fresh tomatoes, baby chicken. $$$$$ 🍷🍷🍷

○ ★ **REIDY'S**—22 East 54th Street (near Madison Avenue)—753-2419—This tiny little Irish bar/restaurant made history when it successfully fought powerful developers who wanted to wipe it from the face of 54th Street and put up a skyscraper. The food is nothing special (chops, Irish corned beef, and such) but this is a warm little corner of Manhattan as resilient as it is vital after all these years. Amex and Transmedia only. $$$ 🍷

★ ★ **PISCES**—60 East 54th Street (near Park Avenue)—753-4441—A pleasantly innocuous seafood restaurant run by the former owners of Seafare of the Aegean, so the best tack to take is to choose the Greek seafood specialties here: shrimp Santorini, red snapper Crete, sea bass Mykonons. The premises are gaily decorated with a colorful mural. Skip the desserts. $$$½ 🍷🍷

★ ★ ★ **LELLO**—65 East 54th Street (near Park Avenue)—751-1555—This handsome room attracts a well-heeled clientele who likes the light Italian cuisine served here amidst glittery decor. The carpaccio is excellent, as are all the pastas. Pretty good desserts too. Pasta primavera, scampi infernale, red snapper. $$$ 🍷🍷🍷

★ ★ ★ ½ **LESPINASSE**—2 East 55th Street (off Fifth Avenue in the St. Regis Hotel)—753-4500—The renovation of the grand old St. Regis has been brought off with commendable respect, including the return of Maxfield Parrish's King Cole mural to the King Cole Bar and the installation of a dignified, formal dining room named Lespinasse under the sure direction of Tony Fortuna. The gray and beige room could use some color and brightening, but chef Gray Kunz's food has plenty of both. He is a stunning provocateur in dishes that will surprise you and inspire other chefs. His cooking techniques bring out the best in his ingredients and his food seems more delicious than ever. Desserts, on the other hand, are design exercises without complementary flavor. Oxtail salad with fennel, fried lobster tail with cucumbers and sauce crustace, lamb chop with eggplant tart and curry-carrot juice. Fixed price menus at $47 and $60. A la carte $$$$$ ♈♈♈

★★★½ **LA CÔTE BASQUE**—5 East 55th Street (near Fifth Avenue)—688-6525—A Manhattan institution founded by the legendary Henri Soulé, La Côte Basque flourishes under chef/owner Jean-Jacques Rachou, and boasts a very faithful clientele. The place is quite glamorous—butter-colored walls, Riviera murals, dark beams, a glittering bar—but the greeting at the door may be indifferent to newcomers, and service abrupt. The food, however, is classic, ornate, satisfying, and well presented. Although the wine cellar here is one of NYC's finest, with many a fine and rare claret, most white wines are listed without either a vintage or producer, making the selection process cumbersome. Saucisson chaud, supreme de volaille Gismonda, veal chop with wild mushrooms, quail and sweetbreads in puff pastry, cassoulet of seafood, dacquoise with raspberry sauce, soufflés. Fixed price dinner $55 but far too many supplements. $$$$$ ♈♈♈♈

★★★★ **QUILTED GIRAFFE**—550 Madison Avenue (off 55th Street)—593-1221—Certainly one of the city's most dramatic interiors, a striking amalgam of deco, post-modern and Far Eastern motifs. Indeed, co-owner/chef Barry Wine proffers several creative dishes which are oriental in inspiration, from the wasabi pizza to a multi-course Kyoto style "kaiseki" menu at a whopping $125. Needless to say, at these prices, the place attracts its fair share of wealthy foreign businessmen. For $75 (there's also a $110 degustation menu) you can sample the likes of tuna tartare with peanut pasta, potato risotto with house smoked salmon, sautéed sweetbreads with soba noodles and a caramel soy glaze, or delight in sea scallops with seaweed sauce, or confit of duck with grains and beans. If you still have an appetite after the cheese course, opt for the grand dessert, a medley of sorbets, cakes, custards, and sweets (but that's an extra $10!). Expensive but very extensive wine list. Not for bargain hunters. ▼▼▼▼

★★★★ **SHUN LEE PALACE**—155 East 55th Street (near Lexington Avenue)—371-8844—One of the problems with all Chinese restaurants is their lack of consistency from month to month and year to year. Shun Lee's owner Michael Tong shows what can be effected when restaurateur and customer have the same standards. The result is the most consistently exciting Chinese food in New York from the Peking duck, crispy orange beef, prawns with eggplant, to the beautifully orchestrated banquet dishes. The Cantonese chef is a master of preparations found nowhere else. Scallops and tofu cakes, quail with frogs legs, and Wang's stuffed eggplant. The premises, though cramped, are lively, and the staff can be either helpful or not, depending on your waiter. Nice wine list. $$$$ ▼▼▼

○★½ **P.J. CLARKE'S**—915 Third Avenue (at 55th Street)—759-1650—A throwback saloon, and one of New York's most popular at that. Once you wade past the crowd in the front room bar, a thriving single's hang-out (tip: enter by the side door on 55th Street and skip the throng), you'll find a pleasant dining room in back serving burgers, chile and home fried potatoes. Convenient to Third Avenue cinemas, this is a spot where history looms larger than the cuisine—which has declined marginally of late. The wait for a table can sometimes be agonizing. $$ ♀

★ **AU MANOIR**—120 East 56th Street (near Park Avenue)—753-1447—Time hasn't just passed Au Manoir by; it seems to have leapt over it. This old fashioned French restaurant does have a real charm if only for its artifact status. Onion soup and sole amandine will be on the menu here forever. $$$ ♀

★★★ **RESTAURANT LAFAYETTE**—440 Park Avenue (entrance on 56th Street in the Drake Hotel)—421-0900—The loss of Jean-Georges Vongerichten (who opened his own place, JoJo, q.v.) sent the management of the Drake scurrying to find a replacement who could live up to Lafayette's former repute as one of New York's greatest restaurants. They have found a good one in Marybeth Boller (who worked with Vongerichten). She wisely goes her own way and is very talented, though some of her sauces are quite sweet and inapt. The problem at Lafayette is the unappealing, poorly lighted dining room and prices that only a handful of NYC restaurants dare charge these days—$65 for a three-course dinner. Mille feuille of foie gras, napoleon of sea bass, duck with Swiss chard, all desserts. $$$$$ ♆♆♆♆

★★★ **MITSUKOSHI**—461 Park Avenue (at 57th Street)—935-6444—Located below a Japanese specialty store, this is a fine retreat for excellent Japanese cuisine, especially the soups, sushi, sashimi, tempura dishes, smoked eel and grilled fish of the day. Restful decor in beige and soft lighting, pleasant service by kimono-clad waitresses, and good lunch specials like bento boxes. $$$ ♆♆

★★½ **LE CHANTILLY**—106 East 57th Street (near Park Avenue)—751-2931—Although chef Bruno Chemal has lightened up the kitchen, it still falls prey to occasional inconsistencies. Moreover, the serious look and feel of the place has not changed. Chantilly remains a somewhat sober-minded spot, ideal for a business lunch. But the menu generally brings it all alive with such welcome additions as sweetbread ravioli, guinea hen, paillard of salmon and tarte Tatin. $$$½ ♆♆♆

★★ **MR. CHOW**—324 East 57th Street (near First Avenue)—751-9030—The quality of the service and food have improved as the novelty factor of the place died down some years ago. The striking neo-deco decor stands up well, however. On a recent visit, we were particularly impressed with Mr. Chow's Noodles, Sieu Mai (mushroom) dumplings, and green shrimp. Even the prices don't seem out of line any more. $$$½ ♆♆

★½ **TONY ROMA'S**—400 East 57th Street (near First Avenue)—421-7427—It's called "A Place for Ribs" and that's just what you should go for. Part of a national chain, and the decor shows it, but the food's OK and not expensive. $$ ♀

★★ **PAPER MOON**—39 East 58th Street (between Park and Madison Avenues)—758-8600—A very slick, Milanese-inspired restaurant with a menu that sometimes looks better than it tastes. It nonetheless manages to draw an attractive mid-town crowd. Good for a quick lunch or dinner when the accent is on speed. You can't go too far wrong with their self-serve antipasto, pastas and pizzas. $$$ ♀♀

★★ **AKBAR**—475 Park Avenue (near 58th Street)—838-1717—A pleasant Indian dining room, especially attractive for lunch but, curiously, they do not offer the kind of lunch buffet most Indian restaurants around town do. The food is well spiced and wide ranging. Vegetable samosa, shami kebab, chicken tikka, lamb vindaloo. Friendly service. $$½ ♀

★★★½ **DAWAT**—210 East 58th Street (near Third Avenue)—355-7555—Unquestionably the city's most attractive Indian restaurant, Dawat specializes in authentic and unusual regional dishes. Veteran India watchers make this their second home. First-timers should sample assorted appetizers from "Madhur Jaffrey's Snack Cart". Whether you fancy chicken tikka or tandoori shrimp, fish or goat stew, baked eggplant, green beans in coconut, sag paneer, baghari jhinga or kheer, you will not be disappointed. Try the Taj Mahal beer. $$½ ♀

★½ **TRE SCALINI**—230 East 58th Street (near Second Avenue)—688-6888—This once bellwether Northern Italian restaurant has drifted for so long it doesn't seem to notice it is way off course in pricing, ambiance, food and service. Non-smokers are relegated to a dreary rear room, the staff is negligent and the prices are very stiff. The food ranges from fair (tagliatelle with tomato and red peppers) to quite good (red snapper in cartoccio), but there are more misses than hits, with most dishes just plain dull. $$$$½ ♀♀♀

★★★★★ **FELIDIA**—243 East 58th Street (near Second Avenue)—758-1479—Lidia and Felix

PRICE SCHEDULE

VOLUME DISCOUNTS
Standard editions of PASSPORT retail for $7.95 and are available at bookstores in the Tri-state area or by mail. Bulk orders result in dramatic discounts and can be placed by sending in this order form, by telephone (212) 772-3942 or by fax (212) 535-8174.

CUSTOMIZED EDITIONS
What better premium for your company than a customized, pocket-sized guide to New York's finest restaurants? A customized PASSPORT is a gift item that sets itself apart from all others.

Customized PASSPORTS are imprinted with a corporate logo, graphics or text on the outside front and/or back cover. The inside cover and additional pages can be printed with the copy of your choice. Delivery is approximately three weeks. *Minimum order is 250 copies.* For information and quotes, please fill out the form below and enclose a sample of your letterhead, logo, or camera-ready artwork. Agency discounts on request.

Standard Edition

1 to 24 copies—$7.95	100 to 499 copies—$6.00
25 to 99 copies—$7.00	500 to 999 copies—$5.00
1000+ —price on request	

YES! SEND ME _____ PASSPORTS @ $ _____

*Add $1.00 *per copy* handling and postage for orders of 1–24 copies. For delivery of larger orders telephone (212) 772-3942.
**New York residents must add 8¼% sales tax.

AMOUNT $ _____

☐ Just send me information about ordering custom PASSPORTS

NAME _____

TITLE _____

COMPANY _____

ADDRESS _____

CITY _____ STATE _____ ZIP _____

TELEPHONE _____ FAX _____

Make check payable and mail to:
Passport Press, Ltd., P.O. Box 1003, New York, N.Y. 10021
Tel. (212) 772-3942   Fax (212) 535-8174

PRICE SCHEDULE

VOLUME DISCOUNTS
Standard editions of PASSPORT retail for $7.95 and are available at bookstores in the Tri-state area or by mail. Bulk orders result in dramatic discounts and can be placed by sending in this order form, by telephone (212) 772-3942 or by fax (212) 535-8174.

CUSTOMIZED EDITIONS
What better premium for your company than a customized, pocket-sized guide to New York's finest restaurants? A customized PASSPORT is a gift item that sets itself apart from all others.

Customized PASSPORTS are imprinted with a corporate logo, graphics or text on the outside front and/or back cover. The inside cover and additional pages can be printed with the copy of your choice. Delivery is approximately three weeks. *Minimum order is 250 copies.* For information and quotes, please fill out the form below and enclose a sample of your letterhead, logo, or camera-ready artwork. Agency discounts on request.

Standard Edition

1 to 24 copies—$7.95	100 to 499 copies—$6.00
25 to 99 copies—$7.00	500 to 999 copies—$5.00
	1000 + —price on request

YES! SEND ME _____ PASSPORTS @ $ _____

*Add $1.00 *per copy* handling and postage for orders of 1–24 copies. For delivery of larger orders telephone (212) 772-3942.
**New York residents must add 8¼% sales tax.

AMOUNT $ _____

☐ Just send me information about ordering custom PASSPORTS

NAME _____

TITLE _____

COMPANY _____

ADDRESS _____

CITY _____ STATE _____ ZIP _____

TELEPHONE _____ FAX _____

Make check payable and mail to:
Passport Press, Ltd., P.O. Box 1003, New York, N.Y. 10021
Tel. (212) 772-3942   Fax (212) 535-8174

Bastianich enjoy a well-deserved reputation for staying at the vanguard of all the latest developments in authentic cucina Italiana. They continue to wield tremendous clout nationwide for their unbridled enthusiasm, their attentiveness to detail and their wine consciousness. Their menu reflects this energy: refined but homey, full of delicacy and flavor. The brick and blanched wood interior is attractive and comfortable. Antipasti, mushroom polenta, ziti with lamb sauce, pappardelle with broccoli di rape, krafi (raisin and ricotta-filled ravioli), raviollaci con fungi, pasta quatro staggione, salmon with mustard sauce, calf's liver balsamico, pineapple and strawberries with balsamic vinegar. The spectacular wine list covers a broad spectrum, from classic Barolos and Brunellos to the latest releases from Italy. $$$$$ ♥♥♥♥♥

★ **CAFE NICHOLSON**—323 East 58th Street (between First and Second Avenues)—355-6769— This unique establishment, more reminiscent of a curio shop than an eatery, enjoys the reputation of having been the restaurant of record for the pop set during the 1960's. To this day Mr. Nicholson only opens when the feeling moves him, and it has been known to remain closed for stretches up to several weeks and more. You sit down to a fixed price four-course menu which can include such throwbacks as mini cheese souffle, roast chicken and filet, and chocolate souffle. It's a must see for the adventurous even though the kitchen is hit and miss. $$$$ ♥

★★★ **ROSA MEXICANO**—1063 First Avenue (near 58th Street)—753-7407—Happily we can report that chef-owner Josefina Howard has restored the luster of Rosa Mexicano and seems to be more in evidence than ever. The premises have a casual charm, the margaritas are among the best in the city and the guacamole is nonpareil—have it as hot as you like, because it's made in front of you. Chipotles rellenos, tripe stew, carnitas of pork, enchiladas de pato, various flans. $$$½ ♥

★★½ **MARCH**—405 East 58th Street (between Sutton Place and First Avenue)—838-9393—This beautifully appointed, intimate dining room located on the site of what used to be Brive is still something of an acquired taste. Although we long applauded Wayne Nish for his powerfully flavored provençal food when he was chef at La Colombe d'Or, in this manifestation, his style verges on the unconventional. Barbecue quail is served blood rare—a condition that is admittedly abated by a strong and flavorful sesame sauce—or by a request from the diner that the bird be cooked to his own specification. The same is true for calf's liver. Good lamb canelloni. The wine list contains some interesting selections and several well-priced half bottles. $$$$½ 🍷🍷

★★★½ **HARRY CIPRIANI**—781 Fifth Avenue (at 59th Street in the Sherry-Netherlands Hotel)—753-5566—The return of the Cipriani family to the Sherry-Netherlands was greeted by faithful customers as if they'd never left (in a dispute with management four years ago). The place rings with laughter, graying men in tight suits and gorgeous women in tighter skirts. Like Bellini by Cipriani on Seventh Avenue, this is an outpost of Venice's legendary Harry's Bar, and the food is simple and delicious, but very expensive. Service is affable, but can be rushed. Tagliatelle verde gratinata, risotto with chicken livers, scallops with artichokes, salmon with zucchini fritters, crêpes à la crème. $$$$$ 🍷🍷

★★★★ **MONDRIAN**—7 East 59th Street (near Fifth Avenue)—935-3434—Under the direction of chef Tom Colicchio, this sumptuous spot has evolved nicely over the past year, although like many similar establishments, the economy has taken its toll in terms of reduced volume. The widely spaced, well-appointed seating arrangements still make Mondrian an ideal place for a special evening or a business outing (there's also a stunning private dining room downstairs). Colicchio produces a modern, inventive cuisine—highly refined, delicate in taste. Ragout of clams, foie gras with leeks, tuna and olive tart, salmon and tuna tartare, sweetbreads with salsify, roasted salmon, venison chop, rabbit with roasted garlic and shallots, blueberry tart. $$$$ 🍷🍷🍷🍷

★★★ **LE TRAIN BLEU**—1000 Third Avenue (at 59th Street in Bloomingdale's)—705-2100—Unlike most department store eateries which are a mere convenience, this is a bona fide restaurant. Modelled on a luxury French railroad dining car, and overlooking the 59th Street bridge, it is a refreshing combination of starched white table tops and forest green interior. Crisped shrimp, goat cheese salad, roast quail with sweetbread stuffing. Very reasonable wines. Open until 7:30 PM Mon. and Thurs.; other business days until 4:00 PM. $$ ♈♈

★★ **ZONA ROSA**—211 East 59th Street (near Third Avenue)—759-4444—One of two Mexican restaurants (the other is at 142 West 44th Street) run by the people who also own Bombay Palace. Big and built for high volume, it gets a young crowd that comes for the slush margaritas and basic Mexican fare, now enlivened by some specialties from cooking authority Jane Butel. Service can be slow and the bar crowd can get noisy. Smokers might be seated next to non-smokers. Spinach quesadillas, pork adobado, sizzling fajitas. $$½ ♈

★★★½ **SANDRO'S**—420 East 59th Street (near First Avenue)—355-5150—Nowhere will you find a more ebullient chef than Sandro Fioriti, who bounds ex culina into the simply decorated dining room and slaps down whatever it is that strikes his fancy that night—roast pork alla romana with fennel and rosemary, luscious bruschetta with tomato, and fresh-from-the-oven lemon cookies. The gelati are among the best in the city. There is a menu, but go with Sandro's suggestions and you'll have hearty food full of flavor. (When he is absent, the kitchen's performance may be inconsistent.) Dinner only. $$$$ ♈♈♈

★★★ **MALVASIA**—108 East 60th Street (near Park Avenue)—223-4790—The atmosphere is faintly Mediterranean in feel, and the menu, somewhat enhanced, remains Italian eclectic. Appealing appetizers such as grilled vegetables, frittata with zucchini and tomato sauce, penne with eggplant sauce and ricotta. Enticing main courses include breast of chicken with goat cheese and pesto, breast of duck in mushroom ragout, grilled veal chop, and grilled tuna. Specials such as Sicilian crab cakes. $$$½ 🍷🍷🍷

★★★ **LE VEAU D'OR**—129 East 60th Street (near Lexington Avenue)—838-8133—This bistro has been elevated to institutional status by NYC's French community and francophiles alike. It's animated, crowded and convivial, the kind of place you might find in Paris' 8th arrondissement. Veau D'Or specializes in hearty traditional dishes like steak frites, loin of pork, calf's liver, cassoulet, and cervelle. Delicious tartes. $$$ 🍷🍷

★★ **YELLOWFINGERS**—1009 Third Avenue (at 60th Street)—751-8615—Convenient to Bloomingdale's and perfect for a light bite after a movie. Good Caesar salad, onion rings. An enticing array of entrées ranges from sandwiches like grilled tuna steak with parsley and red onion on focaccia to homemade herbed sausages. Skip the burgers. Nice selection of wines by the glass. $$ 🍷🍷

★★ **CONTRAPUNTO**—200 East 60th Street (near Third Avenue)—751-8616—A winning combination of bright, modern decor and a great view overlooking the bustle on Third Avenue across the street from Bloomingdale's makes Contrapunto an ideal people-watching spot. It also has some exceptional pastas like ravioli with malfatti with lobster and scallops, tagliarini conga do'oro, and solid grilled main courses. End off with a slice of chocolate torte, a cup of espresso, and you have a perfectly nice lunch or a dinner before going to the movies. $$$ 🍷🍷

★★★ **ARIZONA 206**—206 East 60th Street (near Third Avenue—838-0440—Despite its very casual atmosphere and potentially piercing noise level, this remains a dynamic restaurant for its highly seasoned and imaginative Southwestern cookery and its young, handsome crowd. New chef Beth Valley is carrying on the tradition of good taste here, and portions are enormous; they should be, because prices are also quite high. Desserts are somewhat disappointing. Corn bisque with shrimp, lobster tostada salad with chili avocado sauce, red chile chicken and dumpling stew. $$$$ 🍷🍷

★½ **SERENDIPITY**—225 East 60th Street (near Second Ave)—838-3531—Looking as funky as when it opened in the 1960s, Serendipity is as good as its name—a swell little place where you'll find all sorts of surprises, from campy gifts, postcards and paraphernalia to some very tasty food like chili, burgers and scrumptious desserts like frozen hot chocolate. The people who eat here range from Brooke Shields to prom queens, from East Side artists to Scarsdale matrons. $$

★★★½ **CAFE PIERRE**—61st Street and Fifth Avenue —(in the Pierre Hotel)—940-8185—The ultra-glamorous, somewhat fussy interior of the Café Pierre hardly indicates what disciplined, superb cuisine the kitchen is capable of producing. It can be rich, classic, or, since this is a Four Seasons hotel, light and calorie-conscious (see the Alternative Cuisine menu). Executive Chef Franz Klampfer has kept an even keel here, despite chef changes, and the service staff is top-notch. Foie gras with caramelized apples, salmon filet on creamed lentils. Breast of duck with pear sauce. $$$$ ♕♕♕

★★★ **MADAME ROMAINE DE LYONS**—29 East 61st Street (near Madison Avenue)—759-5200—One of the best kept secrets in midtown. Specializing exclusively in omelettes, Madame Romaine offers a dizzying array of choices, like French bacon, olives, croutons, chicken livers. $$$

★★½ **CAPRICCIO**—33 East 61st Street (near Madison Avenue)—759-6684—Two rooms convey completely different moods. One contemporary and businesslike, the other an enclosed garden room. Either way, you'll find above average Northern Italian cooking. Good bruschetta, tomato and mozzarella, ravioli with red pepper sauce. $$$ ♕♕

★★ **540 PARK**—540 Park Avenue (at 61st Street in The Regency Hotel)—759-4100—This is where the "Power Breakfast" began a decade ago, and it's always jammed by 8 AM with prominent members of the business community. At noontime and after 6 PM things aren't quite so lively in this newly decorated dining room, yet that may change with the arrival of new Chef Andrew Pappas, formerly of The Post House. He is expected to enliven the once bland menu with borrowings from his former posting like the popular Cobb salad, roast beef hash, and deluxe burger. Book well in advance for breakfast. $$$$ ♔♔♔

★★★ **IL VALLETTO**—133 East 61st Street (near Lexington Avenue)—838-3939—Luigi Nanni has returned to Il Valletto, and his spirit imbues the place with all that it lost while he was off at the now defunct Da Nanni. The pretty, floral room with its roomy banquettes is still a delight, though the rear room is not nearly so attractive. The food is of very high quality, if somewhat predictable. The captains seem to have lost much of their snobbishness too. Risotto with radicchio, red snapper in cartoccio, all desserts. $$$$½ ♔♔♔

★★★½ **LE PISTOU**—134 East 61st Street (near Lexington Avenue)—838-7987—Jean Jacques Rachou's pastel-colored bistro is an excellent choice for the value conscious. Chef Claude Franques serves up hearty, traditional French fare at prices that are hard to match. The small mirrored space is quite sprightly, and the staff most eager to please. Pistou provençal soup, salad of tomato, mozzarella, and saucisse de Lyon, roasted salmon with red wine sauce, cassoulet Toulouseanne, breast of capon, fresh fruit tarts. Fixed price $19.50 for lunch, $26.50 for dinner. ♔♔♔

★★★ **GINO**—780 Lexington Avenue (at 61st Street)—223-9658—Verging on institutional status, Gino boasts an old guard following, old school Southern Italian Cuisine (hearty and abundant fare such as eggplant Parmesan and admittedly first class ravioli) landmark Scalamandre zebra-patterned wallpaper, and a wine list with more cocktails than claret and Chianti! A throw-back with a crowd of regulars who swear by it. $$½ ♔

★★½ **OLIO**—788 Lexington Avenue (near 61st Street)—308-3552—Lively and smart-looking, this is a good spot for lunch after a morning's midtown shopping, or for a casual dinner. Good brick oven pizzas, pastas such as fettuccine qualio, and grilled fare such as free range chicken breast with pineapple cilantro and jalapeño sauce, or lamb with rosemary and brandy sauce. No credit cards. $$$ 🍷

★★ **BRIO**—786 Lexington Avenue (at 61st Street)—980-2300—This smart and sprightly trattoria provides a satisfying solution to reasonably priced, midtown Italian dining, convenient to Bloomingdale's and Third Avenue cinemas. Appetizers such as polenta con funghi and carpaccio con carciofi run under $9, and main course pastas fall in the $10 range. Pollo con salsiccia e funghi and paillard di vitello alla brio (breaded) are good bets at $16 each. $$$ 🍷

★★½ **DA FIORE**—808 Lexington Avenue (near 62nd Street)—752-4259—For years, as Restaurant Demarchelier, this spot was home to animated dining. Its latest occupant, Da Fiore, has all the potential to rekindle the vitality. A charming interior, replete with an oversized bar and bas relief ceilings, is now home to some serious Italian cooking. Antipasti freddo, linguine with rabbit, bow-tie pasta with sausage and tomato, veal chop with shallots and rosemary, tira misu. $$½ 🍷

★★★ **ALO ALO**—1030 Third Avenue (at 61st Street)—838-4343—Executive chef Matthew Kenney has done miracles with the menu here; if only someone else would do the same with the decibels. This highly popular, whimsically designed trattoria has become a staple with the singles set, and from the sounds of it, most of them appear to work on the trading floor of the stock exchange. Kenney's innovations such as duck pizza with goat cheese and rosemary, marinated artichokes with toasted walnuts and Parmesan, grilled veal chop with mandarin glaze and risotto, seared red tuna with caramelized shallot vinaigrette and crispy beet chips have elevated the once passable food to pleasing new levels. So bring your earplugs and sample the fare. $$$½ 🍷🍷🍷

★★★★★ **AUREOLE**—34 East 61st Street (near Madison Avenue)—319-1660—Despite hard times at the luxury end of the restaurant spectrum, Aureole continues to impress and delight—and to fill up every night. Magnificent floral arrangements against a bas-relief back-drop make this one of the city's most charming restaurants. Chef Charlie Palmer is forever innovating: appetizers like beef ravioli with foie gras, split pea soup with lobster, warm sautéed sweet-bread salad with ginger, or homemade mozzarella with eggplant; entrées such as sautéed calf's liver with cornmeal puffs, thyme roasted squab smothered in a blanket of crisp potatoes, pan seared monkfish with polenta cakes, apple wood cured mallard duck. Desserts are divine, especially the apple Napoleon ginger mousse, or cape blueberry tartlet with lemon verbena. Fixed price $55. ♀♀♀♀

★★★ **MAXIM'S**—680 Madison Avenue (near 61st Street)—751-5111—Maxim's has steered something of a rocky course since its arrival in New York; numerous changes in chefs, and lately, in manage-ment. As a result, it's no surprise that Maxim's has yet to capture the cachet of its Rue Royale original. It's a tad touristy, although the faux Art Nouveau decor comes alive on Saturday night when black tie is de rigeur. With the appointment last year of chef David Ruggiero, the food has improved dramatically (easily better than Paris). Coquille St. Jacques with truffled leeks, shrimp and fresh foie gras, rosace of lamb on a bed of vegetables. Dinnner. Fixed price $68. ♀♀♀

★★ **L'OMNIBUS**—21 East 61st Street (at Madison)—980-6988—The back door—or strictly speaking, the basement—to Maxim's restaurant. Simple brasserie fare, well prepared and relatively inexpensive. Pates, charcuterie platter, sandwiches, salads. Popular. Closed Sunday. Dinner. $35 fixed price. ♀

★★★★ **ARCADIA**—21 East 62nd Street (near Madison Avenue)—223-2900—Now that chef Anne Rosenzweig is firmly ensconced in Arcadia's kitchen, the food has regained its former glory. The dining room, enlivened by the charming, wrap-around, Paul Davis mural is engaging, but the proximity of the banquettes precludes having a serious business meal here. The limited menu changes frequently, and can include the likes of cucumber and buttermilk soup with fresh basil, mushroom sausage with toasted barley, Arcadian Caesar salad, grilled duck with roasted fig and potato and hazelnut croquettes, mustard-crisped crab cakes on a ragout of corn, tomato and basil, grilled rack of lamb with saffron couscous. Fixed price $55. 🍷🍷🍷

★★★½ CA'NOVA—696 Madison Avenue (near 63rd Street)—838-3725—Owner Corrado Muttin and chef Ali Fathalla have sublimated this charming, quite romantic little dining room into one of unique Mediterranean tastes, and this is fast becoming one of the city's more delectable destinations, particulary at lunch when it draws a very chic crowd. Caveat: Both Muttin and Fathallah now run All Seasons out in Quogue, LI, on weekends, so you may want to book Ca'Nova mid-week. Sweet pepper and basil soup, grilled quail with sage and mushroom polenta, rigatoni with eggplant and ricotta, sliced rack of lamb provençal, flan of cheesecake with pistachio cream. $$$$ 🍷🍷🍷

★★ LE RELAIS—712 Madison Avenue (near 63rd Street)—751-5108—A bona fide bistro smack in the middle of one of NYC's most fashionable neighborhoods—and it looks it. While it's true that many come here more for the scene than the food, Le Relais's menu can be as satisfying as the people watching. Vichyssoise, poached salmon, steak frites. Outdoor dining in season. $$$ 🍷🍷

★★★ LE BILBOQUET—25 East 63rd Street (near Madison Avenue)—751-3036—A full four years after Philippe Belgrange defected from Le Relais to open Le Bilboquet, his fashionable patrons are still lining the streets to get a table at lunchtime. Once inside, the decor is very inviting, and the atmosphere redolent of Paris's Rive Gauche. Bilboquet's preparations are simple, but exceedingly well executed. Salad niçoise, chèvre chaud aux lardons, grilled tuna, breast of chicken. No credit cards. No reservations. $$½ 🍷

★★★½ POST HOUSE—28 East 63rd Street (near Madison Avenue)—935-2888—A mock colonial interior peppered with Americana is the scene for a lively and engaging lunch or dinner. It's a perfect place to dine with guests of diverse palates; you can subsist on stand-bys like Caesar salad, crab cakes, the James Beard burger, and sirloin steak, or opt for the likes of venison chile, lobster pot pie, Cajun beef or filet tips. No matter what, don't overlook the addictive French fries and onion rings. And do take advantage of one of the city's finest wine lists. $$$$ 🍷🍷🍷

★★ **JOHN CLANCY'S EAST**—206 East 63rd Street (between Second and Third Avenues)—752-6666—A smart but sedate spot, distinguished by attractive table settings, serves as the uptown outpost of the Greenwich Village original. The menu is basically conservative, with a few ambitious twists such as yellowfin tuna "chile," and Cajun soft-shelled crabs. Graavlax, lobster stew, roasted halibut with balsamic vinegar sauce. Good crème brûlée. $$$½ 🍷🍷🍷

★★★★ **LE REGENCE**—37 East 64th Street (near Park Avenue in the Plaza Athénée Hotel)—606-4647—The kitchen shines especially bright when one of the famed Rostang brothers (Michel or Philippe, who fly in from their respective restaurants in France to cook here on a revolving basis) is in residence, making this very formal, ornate dining room one of the finest spots to sample dramatic French cuisine. In their absence, resident chef Jean Robert de Cavel does an excellent job himself. The widely spaced apart tables make Le Régence an ideal spot for a serious business meal. But make no mistake, this is also a place for serious eating—from the signature lobster ravioli to potato pancake with home-smoked salmon and crème fraîche, goat cheese brik, seafood in phyllo, calamari tart, figs with coulis of fruit and any number of other delicacies you'll not find anywhere else. Fixed price lunch $25.50. Dinner $49.50. 🍷🍷🍷🍷

★★★★ **JOJO**—160 East 64th Street (near Lexington Avenue)—223-5656—We have long thought of Jean-Georges Vongerichten (formerly of the Restaurant Lafayette in the Drake Hotel) as one of New York's most creative chefs, and now that he's got his own bistro—a bustling, compact, two-level townhouse—

he's cooking with obvious exhilaration. JoJo has become one of the hottest tickets in town, thanks to marvelous cuisine at remarkably low prices (no entrée over $19). Downstairs is loud but fun, the upstairs bar a bit cramped, and a rear room intimate but somber. Thanks to the restaurant's instant popularity, reservations may be a problem, and diners are not always seated promptly. Shrimp in spiced carrot juice, wild mushroom soup, salmon in rice paper, grilled chicken with olives, chocolate Valrhona cake. $$$½ ♔♔♔

★★★ **PRIMOLA**—1226 Second Avenue (near 64th Street—758-1775—A contender for the attentions of celebrities and socialites alike, this attractive uptown trattoria also happens to boast an excellent kitchen. Mozzarella, prosciutto and arugula, veal chop, veal scaloppine, salmon, ravioli. $$$½ ♔♔

★★ **AUNTIE YUAN**—1191A First Avenue (near 64th Street)—744-4040—While it remains an extremely sleek-looking and attractive Chinese eatery, the place seems to lack the energy it once possessed. However, you can expect consistently well prepared, if a tad uninspired Shanghai fried dumplings, spring roll, sesame noodles, country chicken and spicy filet. $$$½ ♔

★★½ **JOHN'S (of Bleecker) PIZZA**—408 East 64th Street (near York Avenue)—935-2895—Though the decor is unglamorous (glorified cafeteria status at best) this branch of the classic Bleecker Street pizza parlor churns out some of the best brick oven baked pizza and calzone on the Upper East Side. Take-out too. $½ ♔

★★ **SEL & POIVRE**—853 Lexington Avenue (between 64th and 65th Streets)—517-5780—A somewhat innocuous, though pleasant looking bistro convenient to Bloomingdale's, good for a light lunch or simple dinner. Good patés, omelettes, Sel & Poivre sandwich, grilled tuna, coq au vin. (Pre-theatre prix fixe $21.95.) $$$ ♔♔

★★★ **FERRIER**—29 East 65th Street (near Madison Avenue)—772-9000—A sprightly and sleek-looking bistro has a strong following of good-looking, well-heeled young people who like to commingle here, especially at the outdoor tables. At lunchtime, there's a wide array of egg dishes, including a delicious open-faced omelette with chèvre. At dinner, Ferrier offers a simple but satisfying array of staples: grilled sardines, tomate au montrachet, steak frites, grilled salmon and gigot d'agneau. For dessert, there's crème brûlée, tarte Tatin and profiteroles. A well-selected wine list includes several premium Champagnes, such as Dom Pérignon and Roederer Cristal, priced virtually at cost. $$½ 🍷🍷🍷

★★★★★ LE CIRQUE—58 East 65th Street (near Park Avenue)—794-9292—For many New Yorkers, Le Cirque is the quintessential Manhattan restaurant. A becoming interior, populated by a crowd of glistening regulars—socialites, celebrities and lesser notables. The indefatigable owner, Sirio Maccioni, and talented chef Daniel Boulud have devised a winning formula: a constantly changing, ambitious menu that almost always pleases. Sumptuous luncheon dishes such as eggs over chanterelles and focaccia. Starters like carpaccio of red snapper or sea bass, or grilled langouste, can be followed by superb pheasant, skate, or salmon, alongside gutsy specials like potato galette with chicken livers, ricotta and onion rings, goujonettes of pompano in butter, or chicken fricasee with foie gras and lentils. A multitude of signature dishes like pasta primavera are available on request. Desserts by Jacques Torres are always a delight, from the famous crème brûlée to fantasies like a chocolate "tower" on a city "map." And the ever-expanding, ever-innovative wine list remains one of the city's very best and most moderately priced—full of buys under $25. The $29 lunch is one of NYC's best bargains. $$$$$ 🍷🍷🍷🍷

★★ DAVID K'S—1115 Third Avenue (at 65th Street)—371-9090—This is the latest manifestation to inhabit a site which formerly housed The Safari Grill, and the earlier David K's eatery. We were somewhat disappointed by a surfeit of nursery noodles, egg dishes. Try hand rolls, Peking chicken, and spicy dumplings. Pricey wine list. $$$$ 🍷🍷🍷

★★½ JAVA—1115 Third Avenue (entrance on 65th

Street)—935-8888—This vast space has variously housed Café Marimba, David K's Café and Gérard's Place (all within a few years). Java continues to show great promise, although it has yet to really catch on. A Thai restaurant headed up by seasoned restaurateur Michael Ngai in partnership with David Keh, Java deftly balances traditional and contemporary dishes. Excellent barbecued herbed quail with sesame soy sauce, grilled prawns java, Balinese chicken satay, grilled red snapper, Semar's brisket of beef, prawns and scallops in Thai coconut crème. $$$ 🍷

★★★★ SIGN OF THE DOVE—1110 Third Avenue (at 65th Street)—861-8080—The lavish decor—heavy on brick arches, mirrors, and statuary—is all that remains of Sign of The Dove's former touristy and profligate image. For a number of years, the kitchen has been on an upswing with Andy D'Amico in the kitchen, and now Sign of the Dove has emerged as a very serious place to dine. Farfalle with braised rabbit, gateau of raw marinated salmon, Maine sea scallops with eggplant relish, beet ravioli with morels, steamed halibut wrapped in spinach with braised leeks, grilled Muscovy duck breast with savoy cabbage, grilled salmon marinated in charmoula. Fixed price $52.50 or à la Carte. (For a less expensive alternative, sample the delectable bar menu.) $$$$$ 🍷🍷🍷

FIFTY-FIRST TO
SIXTY-FIFTH STREET (WEST)

★★★ LA CITÉ—120 West 51st Street (near Avenue of the Americas)—956-7100—An opulent café that rivals Paris' best in feel, presided over by chef Frederic Perrier. Under his direction, La Cité (and its less expensive Grill) finally achieves what one expects from bourgeois French cooking. His foie gras in honey brioche is terrific, his torte Lyonnaise wondrous, the steak frites perfect, and his floating island a great comeback dish. Couple this with a generous selection of out-of-the-ordinary French bottlings, and you've got a good, though somewhat expensive spot for lunch, pre-theater or business dinner. $$$$ 🍴🍴🍴

★★★ **PALIO**—151 West 51st Street (near Seventh Avenue)—245-4850—An exasperating restaurant because it is so inconsistent. The downstairs bar with Sandro Chia mural is enchanting, and the formal upstairs dining room extremely handsome. Service can be professional or downright amateurish. And chef-owner Andrea Hellrigl's food can manifest extraordinary flair or puzzling mediocrity. Very good pastas as a rule, but some fish preparations are truly nondescript. Desserts have always been standouts. Roasted baby Cornish hen, braised oxtails, agnolotti with ricotta, lasagne with white beans, chocolate polenta. $$$$$ 🍴🍴🍴🍴

★★★★★ **LE BERNARDIN**—155 West 51st Street (near Seventh Avenue)—489-1515—This commodious and elegant dining room has dazzled the most demanding seafood lovers since its debut nearly six years ago. With his light, flavorful sauces and tasteful creativity, Gilbert LeCoze is a true master of form and substance, while his sister, Maguy, greets well-heeled customers with flair. The service is impeccable. The wine list is extremely good, alough expensive, with many a rarity. Creative first courses such as oysters with truffle cream, black bass tartare with caviar, marinated cod with juniper ginger, and shrimp and basil beignets delight. The fish carpaccios are excellent. Poached halibut with rosemary and onion confit vies with another version prepared with capers and a warm vinaigrette. Alternatively, try the herb crusted codfish, or the trademark roasted monkfish with cabbage. Leave room for the fabulous desserts. Caveat: The LeCozes are opening a restaurant in Florida, so their attentions may be focused elsewhere this fall. $$$$$ 🍴🍴🍴

★★★ **BELLINI BY CIPRIANI**—777 Seventh Avenue (corner 51st Street)—265-7770—The West Side outpost of the Cipriani family's legendary Harry's Bar. The captains are suave, and the food is incomparable Cipriani, which is to say, simple, flavorful and wholesome. Go for the fixed price menus (about $37) or otherwise pay dearly. The house wines are light and dependable. The list proper is pricey; the bellini cocktail costs eight bucks! Spinach cannelloni, tagliardi with duck ragu, lemon meringue tart. $$$$ ♀

★★½ **TRIONFO**—224 West 51st Street (near Eighth Avenue)—262-6660—A bright, sunny little Italian restaurant with good prices and good ingredients. Breads are homemade, and the antipasti are terrific and worth a meal on their own. Ask owner Rosario for guidance on the specials. Good place for pretheater. $$$½ ♀♀

♡ ★★★★ **"21" CLUB**—21 West 52nd Street (near Fifth Avenue)—582-7200—One of the most famous restaurants in the world, the "21" Club opened originally as a speakeasy during Prohibition and flourished well into the 1980s when it entered a decline. New owners and a dramatic renovation in 1987 brought about a major turnaround. Under Ken Aretsky, "21" is re-asserting its fame once again. Eminences grises Jerry Berns and Pete Kriendler are as energetic as ever, and the place looks just great. Sommelier William Phillips presides over a spectacular 50,000 bottle wine cellar and a 500 entry list. Chef Michael Lomonaco is sensibly marrying tradition to the finest ingredients to keep the menu in sync with the best American classicism has to offer, and as an added option, his "trim menu selections" are a painless way to lose weight. Grilled duck sausage with black currants, crabcakes, filet of sole and tomato, the "21" burger, lemon meringue pie. Reduced price after-theater specials offered from 10:00 p.m. $$$$$ ♀♀♀♀

★★★ **BOMBAY PALACE**—30 West 52nd Street (near Fifth Avenue)—541-7777—You can't depend on the kitchen to produce fine Indian cuisine every night, but when it does, the results are the best in NYC, with wonderful fragrance and spices. The premises have been refreshed, but service can still be stultifyingly slow. Tandoori dishes, all breads, butter chicken, vegetable thali, rasmalai. $$$ ♀

★★ **CESARINA**—36 West 52nd Street (near Fifth Avenue)—582-6900—Good looking and rather glamorous, Cesarina has little else going for it, especially

81

at prices that are very high and a wine list on which there is almost nothing worth drinking under $30. Service is good, but food comes out almost too fast. Best thing to do is order "misto paste"—four different pastas on one plate—and call it a night. $$$$½ ☐

★ **SAM'S RESTAURANT**—152 West 52nd Street (near Seventh Avenue)—582-8700—An American grill with a hip attitude that doesn't hold up under scrutiny. Owners Mariel Hemingway and her husband, Steve Crisman, apparently spend most of their time back in Ketchum, Idaho. Sam's has a Southwestern feel but the food is no big deal, and the kitchen can even muff a simple steak. However, the brick-oven pizzas are first-rate. $$$ ☐

★★½ **GALLAGHER'S**—228 West 52nd Street (near Broadway)—245-5336—This is the best of the West Side steakhouses with a lot of tradition and Broadway razzle-dazzle about it. The place has always been a big sports figures hangout, and there are photos of all the great ones on the walls. The meat—unquestionably fine aged Prime—hangs in the window, and the whole place buzzes with masculine guffaws. This is an enticing place, especially before or after theater. Stay with the steaks, lobster and cheesecake and you'll be happy as a clam. $$$$ ☐

★★ **VICTOR'S CAFE 52**—236 West 52nd Street (near Broadway)—586-7714—Snazzy in a downtown Miami sort of way. Cooking is much better than it used to be, with abundant portions of crisp pork, plantains, and even a "Roberto Duran Victory" steak. Good fun. $$$ ☐

★★½ **CHINA GRILL**—52 West 53rd Street (off Avenue of the Americas)—333-7788—It began and largely remains a California transplant in the style of Wolfgang Puck's Chinois on Main. This handsome, kite-festooned dining room is the first to have found a successful formula for filling the vast ground floor of the CBS "Black Rock" building. Of late, however, China Grill has become a bit formula itself, and one has the feeling that the kitchen simply coasts on the tried and true. Nevertheless, there is nothing to fault in the calamari salad, deep fried parsley and spinach, grilled Mandarin beef, grilled free range chicken with ginger. Good for pre-or post-theater dinner. Can be noisy. $$$ ♟♟

★★½ **GRILL 53**—111 West 53rd Street (near Avenue of the Americas in the Hilton Hotel)—265-1600—A place that should be better known to those who like finely cooked American food, and enjoy very good jazz, which is offered here most nights of the week. The spacious dining room is handsomely appointed, the staff a bit creaky, and the prices well thought out. Tomato soup, sirloin steak, veal chop, tuna steak. $$$$ ♟

★★★★ **REMI**—145 West 53rd Street (near Seventh Avenue)—581-4242—Over the past year Remi has delivered on its early promise to become one of NYC's finest Italian restaurants, buoyed by inter-architect Adam Tihany's spacious, grand interior (and a new outdoor patio) and chef Francesco Antonucci's bright, colorful but never extravagant cooking, which is based on Venetian traditions. From antipasti through dessert cookies and grappas, this is the kind of restaurant that defines Manhattan's genteel image. Bigoli with wild mushrooms, goose carpaccio, gnocchi with tomato, all desserts. Creative wine list. $$$$ ♟♟♟

★★½ **DA TOMMASO**—903 Eighth Avenue (near 53rd Street)—265-1890—A very personable Italian restaurant with good prices and big portions. The premises are nothing elegant, but the service staff couldn't be nicer, and the food, like linguine with black olives, shrimp and prosciutto in a light orange sauce, scallopine with artichokes, and rack of lamb, is dependable and good. $$$$ ♟♟

★★★½ **AQUAVIT**—13 West 54th Street (near Fifth Avenue)—307-7311—A splendid looking Scandinavian restaurant set in Nelson Rockefeller's former townhouse, with high ceilings and waterfall, three levels, a smorgasbord bar, a wonderful selection of iced aquavits, and some delicious food. A unique Manhattan spot, particularly good for a business lunch or dinner prior to a MOMA opening. (Do specify where you wish to be seated when making a reservation; otherwise you might be placed in a dull, low, ante-room beside the smoking section.) Assorted herring, Arctic venison in juniper and apple sauce, good halibut, and salmon. Swedish pancakes. Fixed price $60, but pre-theater dinner in the café at $19 or in the dining room at $38 is a very good deal. ♔♔♔

★★★ **RESTAURANT RAPHAEL**—33 West 54th Street (near Fifth Avenue)—582-8993—A lovely, romantic and appealing French restaurant (with al fresco dining in summer) run by Raphael and Mira Edery, who welcome every customer with gracious enthusiasm. Although the kitchen has undergone several changes, the Ederys strive to maintain high standards. Snails with tomato concasse, julienned jerusalem artichoke, tuna with tapenade, wild mushroom risotto, apple tart. This is also a good spot for a business lunch, or a meal before or after an exhibit at the nearby MOMA. Closed Sunday. $$$$ ♔♔♔

★★½ **BANGKOK CUISINE**—885 Eighth Avenue (near 54th Street)—581-6370—New York hasn't the number of good Thai restaurants many smaller cities have, but Bangkok Cuisine is one of the oldest and best. It doesn't look like much—rather dark and barebones with a fish tank in the dining room—but the food is delicious and as hot as you can stand it on request. The pad thai noodles and shrimp is a great dish here, as is the crispy mee krob noodles and the whole fried fish. $$½ ♔

★★★ **ADRIENNE**—700 Fifth Avenue (at 55th Street in the Peninsula Hotel)—903-3918—Since high-profile chef Gray Kunz left Adrienne to go to Lespinasse (q.v.), the Peninsula Hotel dining room has limped along without much attention. But new chef Adam Odegard has brought his own, less eclectic style to this spacious restaurant overlooking Fifth Avenue with dishes like tuna on risotto with crisp, fried greens, prawns on soba noodles, and banana tartlet. Service is excellent and very attentive. There's also an adjoining bistro that's a good spot for lunch. $$$$ ♔♔♔

★★★½ **MICHAEL'S**—24 West 55th Street (near Fifth Avenue)—767-0555—One of the true progenitors of

California restaurant style, Michael McCarty has replicated the look and feel of his Santa Monica namesake dining room on 55th Street—the same pale colors, the same modern artwork, the staff attired in pink Oxford cloth shirts and khaki slacks, and the same sunny cooking effulgent with salad greens. If the food no longer tastes quite so revolutionary, it is still very good indeed and portions are generous—they should be, given that it's not difficult to spend $50 per person here before dipping into the well-conceived, but pricey wine list. Cream of asparagus soup, gravlax with mustard sauce, roasted quail with wild rice and creamed onions, grilled saddle of rabbit, scallops in a chardonnay cream sauce, chocolate cake. $$$$$ ♥♥♥♥

♡ ★★★★★ **LA CARAVELLE**—33 West 55th Street (near Fifth Avenue)—586-4252—"Le Tout New York" flocked here in the 1960s when protegés of the legendary restaurateur Henri Soulé debuted what would become a bastion of haute cuisine. Thirty-one years later, present owner André Jammet (himself the scion of Paris' Hotel Bristol founding family) has admirably assured a graceful balance of classic and modern. With its beautifully restored Jean Pagès murals and peach banquettes, La Caravelle remains a quintessentially romantic spot. New chef Tadashi Ono has added refreshing Oriental nuances that keep La Caravelle at the top of the city's dining experiences. Crabmeat in a gazpacho sauce, duck filled ravioli with cilantro consommé, snails with fennel and cous cous, marinated fluke, shrimps and scallops lasagne, grilled smoked salmon with mushroom emulsion, crispy duck with cranberries, parfait nougatine, melon sorbet, chocolate surprise. Service is exemplary. Prices are very fair, à la carte at lunch, a pre-theater dinner at $37, and a $54 fixed price dinner. ♥♥♥♥

★★½ **ELDORADO PETIT**—47-49 West 55th Street (near Avenue of the Americas)—586-3434—A truly striking modern decor makes this Barcelona import an ideal spot to take your most stylish clients. The walls simulate Spanish leather, the lighting is discreet, and the service staff cordial. Would that the food had more snap to it. It still seems too refined for what you expect of Spanish cuisine, despite a shake-up in the kitchen, and there's not much depth of flavor in dishes like stuffed guinea fowl, cabbage stuffed with cod, or even the gazpacho. The desserts, though, are rich and flavorful. $$$$ 🍷

★★½ **CORRADO**—1373 Avenue of the Americas (near 55th Street)—333-3133—A smart looking trattoria in the Milanese style. The kitchen seems to have regained the touch it lost when partner Corrado Muttin moved on (Ca'Nova q.v.). The restaurant serves up a pleasing array of reasonably priced pastas such as fusilli Siciliana or rigatoni basilica, plus tuna gravlax, grilled red snapper with sun dried tomatoes and grilled polenta, seared sea scallops with corn, peppers and basil, tiramisu. Corrado's proximity to Carnegie Hall, and its late-night hours, make it a good after-theater spot. $$$ 🍷🍷🍷

★½ **CARNEGIE DELI**—854 Seventh Avenue (at 55th Street)—757-2245—A stereotypical New York delicatessen: crowded and noisy, with service that is both gruff and brisk. You are seated cheek to jowl with your neighbor, and choose from a satisfying array of humorously described entrées such as "Carnegie Haul" (triple decker sandwich with pastrami, tongue, and salami), "Nova on a Sunday" (smoked salmon, sturgeon, and cream cheese), "Hamalot" or "Beefamania"—plus standbys like franks, burgers, and "Egg-stravaganzas." No credit cards. $ 🍷

★ **JOSE SENT ME**—253 West 55th Street (near Broadway)—246-3253—Upstairs Tex-Mex eatery with cramped tables, good bar, and large portions that will not change your ideas on Tex-Mex too radically, but it's convivial and open seven days a week, which in this neighborhood is quite a boon. $$ 🍷

★★ **ROMEO SALTA**—30 West 56th Street (near Avenue of the Americas)—246-5772—Every out-of-town business man knows about Romeo Salta; every out-of-town business woman knows better Italian places. You'll have a fine enough meal here. The decor is given to wrought iron and peasant paintings.

The food is an amalgam of Northern Italian cliches, with some good pastas interspersed. $$$$ ☝

★★ **NICOLE'S**—870 Seventh Avenue (at 56th Street in the Omni Park Central Hotel)—765-5108—This place has the charm of a real Alsatian brasserie right down to the fixtures, and you can get some good items like cassoulet, choucroute and a platter of oysters. No question it gets a tourist/convention crowd, but it's a good pre-or after-theater spot. But it's still a hotel dining room with all that means about service. $$$ 🍴

★½ **TRATTORIA DELL'ARTE**—900 Seventh Avenue (between 56th and 57th Streets)—245-9800—This is what you get when interior designers open an Italian trattoria—a mix of color, loudness, and blandness. The controversial and much publicized decor consists of gargantuan wall hangings of the human anatomy, and after three courses, the joke wears thin. The food ranges from O.K. for lunch to dreadful for dinner—sodden gnocchi, dreary rabbit stew, salty monkfish. Go before or after theater for the thin crusted pizzas and antipasti. $$$½ 🍴

★★½ **PATSY'S**—236 West 56th Street (near Broadway)—247-3491—A bastion of Southern Italian cooking, Patsy's is a good example of consistency and dedication. The decor has been lightened in recent years, but the celebrity photos still form a gallery of stars—Frank Sinatra, Paul Simon, Liza Minnelli, Charleton Heston and others—who really do eat here and even protested publicly when a local food critic lambasted the place in print. You'll certainly not leave hungry and you'll find the gutsy pastas and entreés to your liking, from the wonderful antipasto of sausage, mozzarella and eggplant to the baked rigatoni sorrentino to the garlicky chicken scarpariello. A good spot before the theater or afterwards, and ideal for a quiet midtown lunch. $$$½ 🍴

★½ **MAURICE**—119 West 57th Street (in the Parker-Meridien Hotel)—245-7788—Having tried everything from nouvelle cuisine to hearty Alsatian fare to fill its overdecorated dining room, Maurice has now decided to go "downscale" with an overly creative chef named Marc Salonsky (formerly of Petrossian) who seems to cook by directive of management—not too rich, not too much seasoning, watch the cream and butter, hold the salt!—and the results are bland. The bill can also add up easily. $$$$$ ♈♈♈

♺ ★★½ **RUSSIAN TEA ROOM**—150 West 57th Street (near Seventh Avenue)—265-0947—Justly famous for its longevity, its polished Imperial Palace decor, and its endless parade of celebrities (a scene from the movie Tootsie was filmed here), the RTR is legendary and well it should be. Of course, if you're not Dustin Hoffman or Luciano Pavarotti, you'll probably not get an "A" table downstairs, but the food upstairs tastes just the same. The menu has improved measurably over the last few years, since noted chef Jacques Pepin began consulting here and the imported Russian bread is irresistible. Blini with caviar, borsch, strawberry kissel, blinitchkis. $$$$½ ♈♈♈

★ **HARD ROCK CAFE**—221 West 57th (near Broadway)—459-9320—People don't come here for dinner or lunch as much as they do for a lift. Decor aptly consists of a guitar collection belonging to celebrated musicians. Music blares from noon until the wee hours. The crowd is very young, birthday parties are being celebrated constantly, and don't leave without buying a t-shirt or two for your niece in Des Moines. Good burgers and sandwiches. $½ ♈

★★ **LE BAR BAT**—311 West 57th Street (near Eighth Avenue)—307-7228—Joyce Steins, who also runs the tremendously popular Cafe Iguana, has done it again with a spoof-like twist on the Trader Vic's theme, featuring Vietnamese food of commendable (if high volume) quality. The whimsical decor must be seen to be believed—hanging lighted oversize bats, red satin banquettes, beaded curtains. The bar is smoky, the cocktails fanciful, there is a dance floor downstairs and the music never lets up. The crowd is equally loud and on the make. A medley of appetizers such as Vietnamese spring rolls, sugar cane shrimp, calamari and satés is a meal in itself. Or consider such entrées as lobster in a clay pot, chicken salad, grouper in banana leaves. $$$ ♈♈

★½ **ANCORA PRONTO**—8 West 58th Street (near Fifth Avenue)—308-7100—When the original Pronto opened on 59th Street in the '70s, it signaled a new wave in Italian trattorias. Sadly, the newly opened Ancora Pronto is just a throwback, and quite commercial at that. Although the staff is among the most accommodating you'll find anywhere, for the moment, the kitchen lacks direction. Bland Caesar salad, fried calamari, veal cutlets. $$ 🍷

★★★★ **MANHATTAN OCEAN CLUB**—57 West 58th Street (near Avenue of the Americas)—371-7777—A sleek and stylish interior—adorned with Picasso ceramics—makes this two-tiered restaurant one of the most attractive spots for seafood dining. Chef Jonathan Parker adds wonderful specials each night, while maintaining traditional favorites. Scallops and squid with scallions on pasta, monkfish with lentils, rosemary crusted red snapper, plus standbys like glistening fresh oysters, good poached salmon, grilled swordfish, filet of sole, blackened red fish, warm chocolate tart. $$$$½ 🍷🍷🍷🍷

★★ **JEAN LAFITTE**—68 West 58th Street (near Avenue of the Americas)—751-2323—A slightly Americanized version of a French brasserie—close-fitting banquettes and period movie posters—which draws a lively crowd both at lunch and dinner. While the food can be inconsistent, on a good day the kitchen is capable of turning out fine roast lamb, calf's liver, and steak tartare. Skip the salade Jean Lafitte. $$$½ 🍷

★★ **MESON BOTIN**—145 West 58th Street (near Seventh Avenue)—265-4567—Meson Botin has been around for ages and is very old-fashioned. Nevertheless it does pretty well with the standards of Spanish food, and the swords-and-shields decor is fun. Worth a lunch of shrimps in garlic or paella. $$$ 🍷

★★★ **PETROSSIAN**—182 West 58th Street (at Seventh Avenue)—245-2214—This slick and stylized deco outpost of Paris' famed caviar purveyor is no longer just an emporium for beluga, ossetra, and sevruga (although $160 will snare 30 grams of each, plus pressé blinis and smoked salmon). Thanks to the arrival of chef Rick Laakkonen, the menu has been ambitiously enlarged. For the traditionalist, consider his "teasers"—canapé-size portions of smoked sturgeon rolls, smoked eel with cucumber, and smoked salmon. There's good duck paté, eggplant terrine, and cod cheeks, plus tuna with chanterelles, prawns and frogs' legs with couscous, even loin of lamb. Don't miss the nougat glacé. For a theater outing, or an exotic lunch or dinner, the "expanded" Petrossian is a good, albeit pricey, bet. $$$$$ 🍷🍷🍷

★★½ **THE EDWARDIAN ROOM**—59th Street and Fifth Avenue (in the Plaza Hotel)—759-3000—The splendor of the Edwardian Room is unmatched now that this dowager dining room has been restored to its former grandeur. Executive chef Kerry Simon strives to balance standard continental dishes with some new ideas that are lighter and more modern, like salmon tartare with curry oil or roast duck with lentils and mint and a spectacular dessert of banana slices with an coconut ice cream. For a romantic twilight dinner, this is a wonderful spot. For a quiet, uninterrupted business lunch, there's nothing that comes close. Prices have gotten fearsome however. Pre-theater dinner $42. $$$$$ 🍷🍷🍷🍷

☼ ★★★ **THE OAK ROOM AND BAR**—768 Fifth Avenue (at 59th Street in the Plaza Hotel)—546-5330—The majesty of this legendary, utterly romantic dining room with its oak columns and soft lighting is unique in America, a reminder of what grand dining was once all about. Now, after decades of mediocre food, the kitchen has sublimated the basic steaks, chops and seafood menu to a standard we'd encourage others to match, although we wish prices were lower for this sort of menu. Service is gracious and attentive; even the pianist shows a remarkable talent for discreet entertainment. The Oak Room Bar is as lively (and smoky) as ever. Crabmeat Imperial, chateaubriand for two, swordfish with fresh shrimp, chocolate mousse cake. $$$$$ 🍷🍷

★★½ **MICKEY MANTLE'S**—42 Central Park South (near Sixth Avenue)—688-7777—You can practically conjure up the whole scenario before even setting foot in this fun mid-town eatery. Oversized television screens throughout tuned to—what else—baseball games past and present. Lots of ball club paraphernalia—bats, gloves, uniforms, etc. The food is hearty and portions—be they burgers, fries, or salads—are very large. What's more, Mickey Mantle himself actually sets foot in the place from time to time. Great for kids, little and large. $$$½ 🍷🍷

★ **RUMPELMAYER'S**—50 Central Park South (near Avenue of the Americas)—755-5800—This is where good New Yorkers used to take their senior prom dates—decades ago. It's still a reliable stand-by worth trying for sandwiches and light fare and, most of all, soda fountain delectables. Ideal for children, but you probably won't get out without buying a very expensive stuffed animal. $ 🍷

★★ **THE JOCKEY CLUB**—112 Central Park South (in the Ritz Carlton Hotel near Sixth Avenue)—664-7400—Given the handsome club-like interior—paneled walls and attractive period paintings, you'd expect a menu replete with chops and roasts. Instead, there's a serious attempt at creating ambitious, contemporary fare—smoked prawns in a peanut and mustard fruit sauce, figs stuffed with chevre, breast of free range chicken, scallops over a bed of spinach, bitter sweet chocolate mousse. However, the kitchen has yet to fully master the task, and the disjointed service is not equal to any club or restaurant's standards. Good Chardonnay collection. $$$ 🍷🍷

★★★★★ **SAN DOMENICO**—240 Central Park South (off Columbus Circle)—265-5959—A bellwether restaurant and a replication of the famed namesake in Imola, Italy. Its influence on Italian cooking in the United States has been enormous, and owner Tony May is one of the most knowledgeable men in his field. Chef Theo Schoeneger has an extraordinary sense of flavors and nuance that show in every dish, right down to desserts. The premises are stylish but not overly formal, jarred only by orange tablecloths. The wine list assembled by Giorgio Lingero is one of the finest in the city. Foie gras à Veneto, clams with leeks on bruschetta, risotto with beef juices, pasta with squid, spaghettini with zucchini flowers, rack of lamb, lobster fricassée, apple tart with lemon ice cream. Lunch $35. $$$$$ 🍴🍴🍴🍴🍴

★ **THE GINGER MAN**—51 West 64th Street (off Broadway)—399-2358—There's little to recommend the food at the Ginger Man—rather humdrum burgers, French fries, and other staples—but its proximity to Lincoln Center across the street makes this an ideal spot to grab a bite before or after the ballet or opera, and you never know who might be coming through the door next—quite possibly a celebrity or a whole corps de ballet. $$½ 🍴

★★★★ **SHUN LEE**—43 West 65th Street (off Broadway)—595-8895—Owner Michael Tong has incorporated black banquettes and exotic dragon lanterns into a dramatic Oriental setting. Shun Lee standbys delight as always: lemon beef, chicken with peanuts and soft shell crabs with black beans. The Shun Lee Café (sort of a restaurant within a restaurant) features dim sum as well as "street food," such as suckling pig and beef congee. The café is quite disappointing by comparison to its parent. $$$ 🍴🍴🍴

★ **SFUZZI**—58 West 65th Street (near Broadway)—873-3700—Sfuzzi is the kind of concept restaurant that is highly marketable, having started in Dallas and now opened branches in Houston and Washington, where this might pass for a trendy Italian trattoria; in NYC it functions as nothing more than a disturbingly loud singles' meetery and waystop on the trek to Lincoln Center. The food is lifeless, tasteless pseudo-Italian fare and the staff bumbling. Go for a pizza after "La Traviata." $$$½ 🍴🍴

SIXTY-SIXTH STREET TO
NINETY-SIXTH STREET (EAST)

☼ ★★½ **7TH REGIMENT MESS**—643 Park Avenue (at 66th Street)—744-4107—Set in the 7th Regiment Armory, this enchanting restaurant is an antique dream, with massive dark wood, a terrific old oak bar, and some of the finest down-to-earth American fare you'll find anywhere—simple roast beef, chicken, turkey, mashed potatoes, and everything that goes with them. And the prices are amazingly cheap. A great place for the family. $$½ ☺

★★ **LE COMPTOIR**—227 East 67th Street—(between Second and Third Avenues)—794-4950—A joint venture mounted by the owners of Le Relais and La Goulue (q.v.), this spirited and attractive bistro has been packed with a trendy crowd from the moment it opened, thanks in part to the principals' restaurant savvy. But the price of success is excessive noise and an intolerable wait for a confirmed table. The menu is generally well-executed and quite reasonably priced. It includes such standbys as salade aux lardons, entrecote au poivre, saumon grillé, profiteroles and crème brûlée. Dinner only. $$$ 🍷🍷

★★½ **LA GOULUE**—28 East 70th Street (near Madison)—988-8169—Splendid turn-of-the-century panelling creates an authentic brasserie feeling unmatched anywhere in the city. Juxtapose the period decor with a thoroughly modern crowd, many sporting the latest designer creations, and you have a very special atmosphere indeed. La Goulue is probably the last bastion of the lunch-time cheese soufflé, but despite a change of chef, at dinner, the results are still mixed. Well selected wine list. $$$½ 🍷🍷

★★ **THE POLO**—840 Madison Avenue (near 70th Street in the Westbury Hotel)—439-4835—Just when The Polo was starting to soar, chef Terrance Brennan left to become chef at Prix Fixe (q.v.), and although his modern style is still a legacy here, chef changes have troubled this kitchen ever since. Appetizers fare better than entrées. Service can be slow. $$$$½ 🍷🍷

★★ **SHELBY'S**—967 Lexington Avenue (near 70th Street)—988-4624—An instant hit with a slightly more junior version of the Mortimer's (q.v.) crowd, this place churns out simple but satisfying food, with an accent on charcoal grilled preparations. A lively bar scene contributes to the inviting atmosphere. Crisp grilled sweetbreads, Caesar salad with calamari, grilled monkfish, Shelby Burger, half roasted

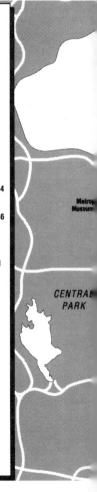

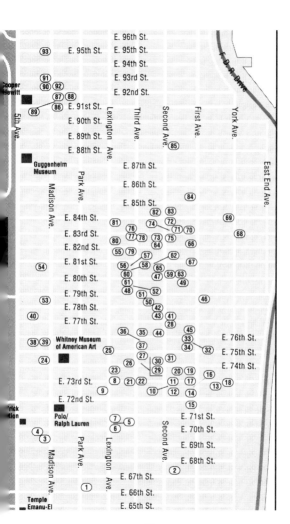

E. 96th St.
E. 95th St.   E. 95th St.
(93)   E. 95th St.
E. 94th St.
E. 93rd St.
E. 92nd St.
(91)
(90) (92)
(87) (88)
(86)   E. 91st St.
(89)
E. 90th St.
E. 89th St.
E. 88th St.
(85)

Cooper Hewitt

5th Ave.

Guggenheim Museum

E. 87th St.
E. 86th St.
E. 85th St.
(82) (83)
(84)
(69)

Madison Ave.
Park Ave.
Lexington Ave.
Third Ave.
Second Ave.
First Ave.
York Ave.
East End Ave.

E. 84th St.
(81) (76) (74) (72)
E. 83rd St. (77) (78) (73) (71) (70)
E. 82nd St. (80) (75)
(55) (79) (64) (66)
E. 81st St. (57) (62)
(54) (56) (58) (65) (67)
E. 80th St. (60) (47) (59) (63)
(61) (49)
E. 79th St. (53) (48) (51) (52)
E. 78th St. (40) (50) (42) (46)
E. 77th St. (43) (41)
(28)
(36) (35) (44) (45)
Whitney Museum (33)
(38)(39) of American Art (25) (37) (34) (32) E. 76th St.
(24) (30) (31) E. 75th St.
(26) (27) (29) (20) (19) (16) E. 74th St.
(23) (8) (21) (22) (11) (17) (13) (18)
E. 73rd St. (9) (10) (12) (14)
(15)
E. 72nd St.
(7) (5) E. 71st St.
Polo/ (6) E. 70th St.
Ralph Lauren
Frick Station
(4) Second Ave. E. 69th St.
(3) (2) E. 68th St.
Park Ave. E. 67th St.
Lexington Ave.
(1) E. 66th St.
Madison Ave.
Temple E. 65th St.
Emanu-El

95

chicken with cheese grits, apple torte with Jack Daniel's. $$½ ♀♀

★★★ **SETTE MEZZO**—969 Lexington Avenue (near 70th Street)—472-0400—An equally lively sibling of Vico, and Vico Madison (q.v.), Sette Mezzo has virtually become the trattoria of record for the Upper East Side smart set. However, the price of popularity can mean a lengthy wait in a cramped corridor for a confirmed table. The appealing menu is similar to Vico's—with such signature dishes as home-made stuffed mozzarella, fried zucchini, red snapper with balsamic vinegar, and penne with sausage and broccoli di rape. The flattened breaded veal chop is another must; alternatively, try the paillard of veal with olives and tomatoes. Good tiramisu and tartufo. The wine list now boasts many unusual Italian estate bottles. Reserve well in advance. No credit cards. $$$ ♀♀

★★★ **LA PETITE FERME**—973 Lexington Avenue (near 70th Street)—249-3272—A cozy French bistro with garden dining in summer, and year-round musical interludes provided by a pair of songbirds. Good hors d'hoeuvres varies, green salad, grilled salmon, roasted chicken. Pleasing wine list. Closed Sunday. $$$½ ♀♀

★★ **ADAM'S RIB**—1338 First Avenue, (near 72nd Street)—535-2112—Now in a bright and cheery location, (especially convenient for a bite apres-Sotheby's) this bastion of Caesar salad, roast beef and hamburgers continues to produce satisfying results. Good Welsh rarebit. $$½ ♀

★★½ **LETIZIA**—1352 First Avenue (between 72nd and 73rd Streets)—517-2244—Although the dining room is rather starkly decorated with terra-cotta tile floors, white-peach walls, and black wood chairs, and the place hasn't actually garnered much of a reputation, Letizia is another of those Upper East Side ristoranti that does an exceptional job of providing very good food on a consistent basis. Service is swift and courteous. Desserts are forgettable. Panzotti with porcini and olive paste, malfatti del ghiottone, pizzocheri Valtellinese, swordfish agrodolce. $$$½ ♀♀

★★★ **MIMOSA**—1354 First Avenue (near 72nd Street)—988-0002—Chef Marilyn Frobuccino (ex Arizona 206) has moved uptown a dozen blocks to the site formerly occupied by Plum Island. While the premises are still somewhat drab, Frobuccino's cheerily eclectic menu (with a California-Italian bias) brings a refreshing touch to the neighborhood. Addicting eggplant dip. Barbecued foie gras with black pepper sauce and brioche, fried cheese with red onions and okra, fettucine with sun-dried tomato, fresh mushrooms and aged goat cheese, percetelli with sardines, Barolo currants, and pine nuts, herb crusted Norwegian salmon with tarama and grilled vegetables, crème brûlée. $$$ 🍷

★★★ **HULOT'S**—1007 Lexington Avenue (near 73rd Street)—794-9800—Hulot's is proof positive that a well-run, attractively decorated neighborhood bistro can withstand the vicissitudes of Wall Street, revolving door chefs and fleeting fads. Owner Gerard Oliver's formula for success consists of friendly service and consistently gratifying preparations. Good lunchtime omelettes, salade niçoise, salade aux lardons. Vegetable terrine, grilled leeks, saucisson chaud, salad of arugula, bacon, roasted potatoes and cheese, roasted baby chicken, flank steak, flourless chocolate cake. $$$ 🍷🍷🍷

★★ **GREEK VILLAGE**—1016 Lexington Avenue (between 72nd and 73rd Streets)—288-7378—An unpretentious, unassuming, but altogether satisfying place to sample traditional Mediterranean fare. You can count on appetizers such as eggplant mousse, dolmas, and taramasalata, plus entrées like moussaka, felafel, and a decent mixed grill. Good baklava. $$½ 🍷

★ **BBQ**—1265 Third Avenue (at 73rd Street)—772-9393—This revolving door space has been home to a steak house and two Italian eateries in the past few years, and now, as its name suggests, it is home to a barbecue emporium. A brimming bar scene and outdoor terrace dining in season prove a major draw. Ironically, barbecued chicken, ribs and burgers play second fiddle to BBQ's fried fare; the vegetable tempura, onion rings and French fries are substantially better prepared. $$

★½ **ALL AMERICAN DINER**—1266 Third Avenue (at 73rd Street)—472-4600—A very safe and sanitized version of the traditional diner, with a sleek, contemporary look. You'll still find proverbial diner classics nonetheless: a bevy of burgers and sandwiches, cold salad platters, eggs and omelets, plus griddle specialties. Cap off the experience with a super sundae. $$ 🍷

★★★ **MILANESE**—1393 Second Avenue (near 73th Street)—570-9270—Residential neighborhoods need more Italian restaurants like this: small, comfy, somewhat sedate, serving up well-executed trattoria fare. Milanese's appetizing fare includes salad of shrimp, scallop and green beans, an excellent Caesar salad, veal scallopini, good pasta specials and rich desserts. Closed Sunday. $$$$ 🍷🍷

★★★½ **FU'S**—1395 Second Avenue (between 72nd and 73rd Streets)—517-9670—A highly popular, slick Upper East Side spot offering a wide variety of Mandarin, Szechuan, Hunan and Cantonese specialties. Fried half moon dumplings, spring rolls, honey baby spareribs, home style chicken, "wonderful taste lover's nest"—sauteed shrimp and scallops. $$½ 🍷

★ ½ **CAMELBACK & CENTRAL**—1403 Second Avenue (at 73rd Street)—249-8380—A pleasant, if innocuous spot for a light lunch or dinner. Simple salads, grilled fare, pastas, plus ambitious specials such as ham and lentil soup and throwbacks like spinach quiche not worth resurrecting. $$½ 🍷

★★ **PETALUMA**—1356 First Avenue (at 73rd Street)—772-8800—This attractive and airy Upper East Side spot has weathered changes in management and in the kitchen, yet remains as popular and inviting as ever. Lots of lightly sauced grilled fare from tuna to chicken share the stage alongside brick oven pizza and pasta specials. $$½ 🍷🍷

★½ **COASTAL CAFE**—1359 First Avenue (at 73rd Street)—472-6204—Much like its noisy older sibling on Amsterdam Avenue (q.v.), this restaurant aspires to Southwest cooking, with an accent on the "catch of the day." The results are hit and miss. Ginger skewered chicken, jalapeño jack and bean nachos, stir fry vegetable tortilla. $$ ☻

★★ **DA NOI**—1394 York Avenue (near 73rd Street)—628-7733—A highly stylized interior replete with marble, chrome and glass contrasts with a menu that is traditional Italian. Assorted antipasti, linguine with bacon and sausage, boneless quail in cognac sauce, sole with leeks, tartufo. $$$ ☻☻

★★ **MALAGA**—406 East 73rd Street (near York Avenue)—737-7659—A casual neighborhood café that has been quietly serving up splendid Spanish especialidades for years. Though the surroundings are a bit dreary by today's standards, delicious chorizo, gambas, paellas, and mariscadas plus a very reasonably priced Spanish wine list more than compensate. $$½ ☻☻

★★★ **COCO PAZZO**—23 East 74th Street (off Madison Avenue)—794-0205—Pino Luongo has had astounding success on the restaurant scene—first at Le Madri (q.v.), then at Sapore di Mare in East Hampton, and now at Coco Pazzo (which means "crazy chef") by serving solid, substantial Italian food in casually chic surroundings. It is no surprise that Coco Pazzo has already garnered a loyal and predictably fashionable following. Chef Mark Straussman is a competent interpreter for Luongo's basic Tuscan repertoire, but volume business can cause inconsistency. Reservations are not easy to come by, and expect a wait. Papa al pomodoro, cotechino sausage, deviled chicken, halibut with pesto, rigatoni with beef, penne with wild mushrooms. The wine list is replete with costly new-wave Italian blends and single crus to the detriment of less expensive selections. $$$$½ ☻☻☻

★½ **VIVOLO**—140 East 74th Street (near Lexington Avenue)—737-3533—A highly popular local eatery. Dark wainscoting creates a sort of clubby, old world feel, which works well on the walls, but appears to carry on into the kitchen where an old-fashioned approach to cooking prevails. Sautéed baby artichokes, Caesar salad (chicken with prosciutto was a tad gummy) grilled swordfish with mustard sauce, strawberries with zabaglione. $$$ ♙♙

★★ **J.G. MELON**—1291 Third Avenue (at 74th Street)—744-0585—This popular neighborhood pub bristles with activity until the wee hours. The casual decor is enlivened by paintings and prints of—what else—the melon in myriad manifestations. Melon's attracts a diverse uptown crowd and gives the first-time visitor an instant slice of uptown life. Excellent bacon-cheeseburgers, chile, club sandwiches and cottage fries. Great bar. Good Bloody Marys and Bullshots. No reservations. No credit cards. $$ ♙

★★½ **VIA VIA**—1294 Third Avenue (at 74th Street)—439-0130—The uptown branch of the sprightly 37th Street trattoria offers virtually the same menu as its mid-town sibling (q.v.). You'll find a variety of moderately priced carpaccios, creative antipasti, pasta such as penne with sun-dried tomato, and grilled fare. There are a dizzying 22 brick oven pizzas ranging from the traditional Margherita to the melanzane—goat's cheese, Parmesan, eggplant, oregano—and "glasnost"—dill cream and caviar (the owner's favorite). $$½ ♙♙

★★★ **MEZZALUNA**—1295 Third Avenue (near 74th Street)—535-9600—Possibly borrowing a note from Melon's next-door, Mezzaluna's walls are decked out with dozens of artful interpretations of the two-handled chopping device after which the restaurant is named. This bristling trattoria is alive until the wee hours and is still populated by a trendy European crowd. Good carpaccio, insalata Mezzaluna, pumpkin tortelloni, pasta specials and superb brick oven pizzas. No reservations. No credit cards. ♙

★ **CAFE LUCAS**—1307 Third Avenue (between 74th and 75th Streets)—744-4978—A lively, retro-looking space featuring a chrome towel bar and brightly colored walls has become the latest hip hangout for the neighborhood. The attraction may well be low prices, and the occasional live jazz combos which perform here, for the simple menu—pastas, pizzas, and "mod courses"—is hardly the drawing card. Cash only. $$ ♙

★★★ **AL AMIR**—1431 Second Avenue (near 74th

Street)—737-1800—A bright and cheery Middle Eastern restaurant that attracts both Upper East Side locals and devotees of Arab cooking from all over. Expect expertly prepared cold appetizers such as tabouli, hummus, baba ghannouj and hot starters like felafel, makanek, and fatayer. As entrées, try the charcoal broiled chich taouk, grilled lamb or gambari. Excellent homemade pastries. $$½ 🍷

★★★★ **CAFE CROCODILE**—354 East 74th Street (near First Avenue)—249-6619—This comfortable and cheery space, situated in an uptown townhouse, serves up ample portions of hearty, Provençal-inspired cuisine, tempered by a smattering of Middle Eastern fare. Presided over by the talented chef Andrée Abramoff (she co-owns the restaurant with her husband) Café Crocodile delivers a menu that is both ambitious and crowd-pleasing—no mean feat. The assorted hors d'hoeuvres make an excellent starter, along with the leek tart, and eggplant with goat cheese. Follow with stuffed capon, chicken with olives, Pernod St. Jacques, or the ever-satisfying couscous. Closed Monday. Amex only. $$$ 🍷

★★½ **CAMPAGNOLA**—1382 First Avenue (near 74th Street)—861-1102—A very pleasing Italian restaurant noted for its antipasti and its decent prices. Most of the food is robust and tasty, making this a good place for a winter's meal. But regardless of season, Campagnolo is a popular spot for an informal night out. Antipasti, orecchiette Caccese, gnocchi al pesto, scallopine alla Sorrentina, lamb chops scottadito. $$$½ 🍷

★★★ **MORTIMER'S**—1057 Lexington Avenue (at 75th Street)—517-6400—For well over a decade, Mortimer's has reigned supreme as watering hole and eatery of preference for Manhattan glitterati (at midday it virtually functions as a private club for ladies who lunch; it fills with an army of notables by night), and, as a result, non-regulars may be treated with indifference. Food has always been simple and good, but of late the menu has been enlivened. Baby Caesar salad, tomato tart, Senegalese soup, twin burgers Mortimer, steak frites, roast chicken, excellent profiteroles. $$$ 🍷🍷

★★ **CIAOBELLA**—1311 Third Avenue (off 75th Street)—288-2555—If you don't take Ciaobella ("hello, beautiful!") too seriously and let yourself get into the swing of things—loosen your tie, sit outside, chat with the pretty girls and handsome guys to either side, and order simply—you'll have a great time and dine well enough on the penne and spicy tomato sauce, tagliatelle with baby artichokes, veal with funghi porcini. The crowd here is easy on the eyes, the prices easy on the wallet. $$$ 🍷🍷

★★ **BRIGHTON GRILL**—1313 Third Avenue (near 75th Street)—988-6663—Brick walls and bent wood chairs create a relaxed and cozy feeling at this Upper East Side eatery which specializes in grilled fare. Salmon, chicken and beef cooked over mesquite are all well-executed, as are the appetizing lunch-time salads. $$$ 🍷🍷

★½ **JIM McMULLEN'S**—1341 Third Avenue (near 75th Street)—861-4700—A smart ladies luncheon spot by day, a highly popular singles hangout by night. The affable Jim McMullen draws a mixed bag of models, sports figures and other attractive types to this cheery uptown spot for simple food such as roast chicken, grilled tuna and the like—a formula that has worked well for over a decade now. $$$ 🍷🍷

★★ **VASATA**—339 East 75th Street (near First Avenue)—988-7166—One of the few remaining Czech restaurants in a neighborhood once full of Eastern European eateries, Vasata is still a solid and friendly little spot where you get good value for the dollar and never leave hungry. Good comfort food. Roast goose, dumplings, apricot crepes. $$$ 🍷

★★★ **LES PLEIADES**—20 East 76th Street (near Madison Avenue)—535-7230—A long-standing favorite of art dealers and collectors because of its proximity to uptown galleries and museums, Les Pleiades serves up traditional French fare in formal and handsome surroundings—red lacquered walls and comfortable banquettes. Service is impeccable. Assiette de charcuterie, celeri remoulade, roast chicken, lamb stew, poached salmon, plus stand-bys like cervelle and cassoulet. Reasonable wine list. $$$ 🍷🍷

★½ **THE THREE GUYS**—960 Madison Avenue (near 76th Street)—628-8108—This is just a coffee shop— simple and cheap—but it is one of the last vestiges of a Manhattan tradition (à la Mayflower Coffee Shop in the old Savoy Plaza Hotel). Prompt, efficient service. Decent club sandwiches and hamburgers. Attracts the Madison Avenue art set. $

★★★★ **IL MONELLO**—1460 Second Avenue (near 76th Street)—535-9310—Owner Adi Giovanetti (he also owns Il Nido, q.v.) was one of the first to elevate Italian cuisine from the veal parmigiana era to the modern age with his light, succulent grilled Tuscan meats, his luscious homemade pastas, and his devotion to the finest Italian bottlings. It all began here at Il Monello (which means "the little rascal"). Adi and his son maintain the service at a high level, and they are very fond of adventurous eaters, so put yourself in their hands. Chicken with funghi porcini, shrimp with Tuscan beans, risotto al Barolo, semi-freddo. Closed Sunday. $$$$ 🍷🍷🍷

★ **CAFE SAN MARTIN**—1458 First Avenue (near 76th Street)—288-0470—This is one of those places that seems suspended in time—a solicitous Maitre D', live piano entertainment, outmoded decor. Yet such is the charm that you still want it all to work. Sadly, with the exception of the chorizo appetizer, there's not much to recommend; both the chicken and seafood paellas were dry and lacking in sustenance. Only the wine list—a fabulous array of vintage Riojas—was truly stellar. Dinner only. $$$ 🍷🍷🍷

★★ **VOULEZ VOUS**—1462 First Avenue (at 76th Street)—249-1776—A very pleasant and attractive neighborhood bistro serving traditional French fare like onion soup, moules marinières, saucisson with lentils, roasted chicken, and steak au poivre. Decent wine list. Open Sunday. $$$ 🍷

★★ **ALBUQUERQUE EATS**—1470 First Avenue (near 76th Street)—734-1600—A lively addition to the East Side Tex-Mex set. Excellent appetizers include chorizo and a "mountain of nachos." Good mixed grill and grilled shrimp. $$ ♀

★★★★ **MARK'S RESTAURANT**—77th Street and
Madison Avenue (in the Mark Hotel)—879-1864—
Chef Philippe Boulot is one of Manhattan's brightest
stars. His technique, acquired via Joel Robuchon and
Alain Senderens, is impeccable, his ideas sound, and
his food full of flavor. Boulot's wife, Susan, does pastries that match up with his menus. At lunch-time,
the place is quiet, but ideal for a business meeting
over a delectable Caesar salad with shrimp quesadil-
los, paillard of chicken or mixed seafood grill.
Signature dinner dishes include lobster baked potato
over a bed of spinach, napoleon of asparagus and
wild mushroom ragout, braised duck leg en civet,
nectarine and blueberry crisp. $$$$$ ♀♀♀

★ **ANTICO CAFFE**—1477 Second Avenue (at 77th
Street)—879-4824—A colorful interior with liberal
borrowings from Mondrian and Miro has become a
popular neighborhood hang-out. The simple Italian
fare is far less innovative than the decor. Caesar
salad, pasta with four cheeses, bocconcini with
prosciutto and peppers, pizza with sausage and moz-
zarella, tiramisù. No credit cards. $$½ ♀

★★ **COCONUT GRILL**—1481 Second Avenue (near
77th Street)—772-6262—An overnight yuppie sensa-
tion, this soothing pastel interior is transformed at
night into a sea of suspenders. The kitchen serves up
simple and somewhat predictable food—a composed
salad of vegetables, dilled cucumber soup, and a
spate of grilled fare. $$$ ♀

★★★ **SIMON'S**—1484 Second Avenue (near 77th
Street)—628-8230—Chef Simon Teng brings two
decade's worth of experience to this sprightly Second
Avenue spot, a veteran of such stellar establishments
as Pig Heaven, David K's and Auntie Yuan. His menu,
based on traditional Chinese delicacies, is extremely
flavorful and innovative, yet maintains a home
cooked touch. Hot and spicy bean sprout rolls,
Szechuan wonton, shredded chicken, General Tso's
chicken, tangerine beef, Hunan Two delicacies (spicy
shrimp and shredded pork in black bean sauce).
$$$½ ♀

★★★ **NATALINO**—243 East 78th Street (between Second and Third Avenues)—737-3771—A gem of a trattoria, tucked away on one of the city's most attractive sidestreets. But unlike a multitude of slick, almost pre-packaged Italian restaurants to open of late, there is nothing formula about this charming, if diminutive spot. Loyal customers (greeted on a first-name basis by the owner) come here for the likes of carciofi fritti, home hewn pastas, stuffed eggplant, breaded veal chop, or specials like chicken pizzaiola. Excellent ricotta cheese cake. What's more, with only a single entrée priced above $16.00, this is clearly a place that represents good value. $$½ ☗☗

★★★ **LUSARDI'S**—1494 Second Avenue (near 78th Street)—249-2020—A delightful neighborhood trattoria, with a cozy interior and very friendly service, which produces superior Northern Italian fare. Good grilled vegetables, grilled smoked mozzarella and radicchio, pasta in pheasant sauce (in season, why not splurge for an appetizer portion of pasta and white truffles for one of the lowest supplements in town—$7). Sautéed salmon, veal sorpresa, red snapper with artichokes. Splendid chocolate cake. $$$ ☗☗☗

★★ **SAINT AMBROEUS**—1000 Madison Avenue (near 79th Street)—570-2211—Attractive Upper East Side trattoria/tea room/take-out with a draped ceiling that creates a pavilion-like effect. Assorted antipasto, good carpaccio, light pasta. $$$$ ☗

★ **THE RAVELLED SLEEVE**—1387 Third Avenue (near 79th Street)—628-8814—A popular post-Prep hang-out that serves up acceptable, if unexiting fare —burgers, steaks and pasta. A lively bar scene remains the prime drawing card. $$ ☗

★★★½ **QUATORZE BIS**—323 East 79th Street—535-1414—A carbon copy of the popular downtown bistro Quatorze, which occupies the space that formerly housed Remi, Quatorze Bis (bis, logically enough, means "twice") brings a touch of Paris's Boulevard St. Germain to 79th Street. Both the menu and the interior design resemble the original establishment (owned by another Peter Meltzer, not the co-author of PASSPORT TO NEW YORK RESTAURANTS). For lunch, there's a highly appetizing prix fixe menu of soup followed by a "tartine" sandwich for $10.50. At dinner, sup on such staples as saucisson chaud, salade aux lardons, creamy paté, coq au vin, steak frites and choucroute garni. You'll also find excellent desserts, plus a very good wine list. $$$½ ♙♙♙

★★½ **L'OUSTALET**—448 East 79th Street (near First Avenue)—249-4920—Veteran New Yorkers will remember this spot once housed the charming Jacques Coeur. In its stead, L'Oustalet serves up hearty bistro fare (escargots, steak tartare, couscous, cassoulet.) Use your imagination with the decor, which though pleasant does not match the culinary expertise. Great for a robust winter meal. $$½ ♙♙

★ **LUKE'S BAR & GRILL**—1494 Third Avenue (between 79th and 80th Streets)—249-7070—A more contemporary looking version of P.J. Clarke's (q.v.) or J.G. Melon's (q.v.) which has yet to develop its own gang of regulars. Worth considering for a quick sandwich or burger, but skip the more elaborate dishes. No credit cards. $½ ♙

★★ **DUE**—1396 Third Avenue (near 79th Street)—772-3331—Owners Mario and Luigi Lusardi (they also own Lusardi's, q.v.) are on the right track here—a handsome, Gwathmey-designed modern trattoria in grays and browns and a menu of good Italian specialties at very welcome prices. The food is not spectacular, but this is a good drop-in place for a moderately priced meal. Crostini di polenta with gorgonzola, risotto with gorgonzola and taleggio, hazelnut and ricotta ice cream. $$$ ♙♙

★★ **SAM'S CAFE**—1406 Third Avenue (near 80th Street)—988-5300—A very popular neighborhood hangout with somewhat ordinary decor launched by "Sam" aka Mariel Hemingway, and her husband (who are rarely in residence). Preparations are simple and healthy, like grilled swordfish, tuna and roast chicken. Less formula in feel than its cross-town branch, Sam's Restaurant located in The Equitable Building. $$$ ♙

★★ **TIRAMISU**—1410 Third Avenue (at 80th Street)—988-9780—Third Avenue is fast becoming the land of the brick oven pizza, but this attractive brick-walled addition to the strip is well worth the visit. In addition to the pizzas, you can also sup on a pleasing array of pasta specials, even Florentine steak. And needless to say, the tiramisu isn't bad either. Good wine list. No credit cards. $$½ 🍷🍷

★★★½ **PIG HEAVEN**—1540 Second Avenue (near 80th St)—744-4887—This place would be great fun if only for its piggy decor—dancing pigs, balloon pigs, all kinds of porcine jokes in the decor. But it's also one of the most interesting Chinese restaurants in America, specializing in barbecued pork and other dishes that will make you wonder what you ever saw in an egg roll. Scallion pancakes, fried pork dumplings, Cantonese suckling pig, three-glass chicken, lobster with ginger. American desserts. Amex and Diners only. $$½ 🍷

★★★½ **SISTINA**—1555 Second Avenue (near 80th Street)—861-7660—The Brothers Bruno run this small Italian dining room with enormous gusto, and the customers have responded by becoming very faithful regulars. The best dishes derive from the Brunos' ancestral region—the Amalfi Coast—so ask what the specials are each night and let them guide you to some real treasures. Well-chosen Italian wine list. Sausage and broccoli di rape, tubettini with shrimp, cappuccino gelato. Amex only. $$$$ 🍷🍷🍷

★★ **ISTANBUL CUISINE**—303 East 80th Street (near Second Avenue)—744-6903—This tiny open kitchen brings a touch of Turkey to the Upper East Side. There's a broad array of traditional appetizers (the hummus, and lamb sausage are especially good), and the usual shishkebob, moussaka and Baklavah—all served up in a homey, casual setting. No liquor license. No credit cards. $$

★★★★½ **PARIOLI ROMANISSIMO**—24 East 81st Street (near Madison Avenue)—288-2391—Surely the most sumptuous Italian restaurant in New York, set in an elegantly decorated East Side townhouse, and presided over by its genial owner, Rubrio Rossi. Parioli boasts a loyal following (the menu is so extensive that several repeat visits are advisable to get a feel for it all). One delights in the likes of fennel tart, ravioli stuffed with goat cheese in a delicate tomato reduction sauce, razor-thin slices of bresaola suffused with white truffle oil, myriad risottos, sautéed Jerusalem artichokes, pheasant filled cannelloni, bistecca Romana in caper sauce, roasted baby chicken with black truffles, superb rack of baby lamb with mustard fruits, and the best cheese tray in the USA. Don't overlook the zabaglione with raspberries or the tira misu. Excellent service. Dinner only. Now open Mondays. $$$$$ ♥♥♥

★★★ **PINOCCHIO RISTORANTE**—168 East 81st Street (near Third Avenue)—650-1513—Exposed brick walls, tin ceiling, candle light and period bric-a-brac create a charming and intimate setting. It's a cozy spot to sample angel's hair pasta with wild mushrooms, sausage and artichokes in oil, boneless breast of chicken in tomato sauce, salmon puttanesca. Good zabaglione and tiramisu. Small but well chosen wine list. $$$ ♥♥

★★★ **ANATOLIA**—1422 Third Avenue (near 81st Street)—517-6262—Faux marble columns, striking abstract light fixtures and a trace of traditional Turkey (an antique samovar and tray) make for an unusual, but very effective setting. Go with an appetite because you'll want to eat at least three full courses. Superb appetizers include zucchini "pancakes" stuffed with feta cheese, dill and scallions, baked vine leaves stuffed with pilav, and Turkish meat and arugula pie. For the main event, try the skewers of grilled quail in grape leaves or "Sultan's bliss"—lamb in a tomato sauce served on a bed of roasted eggplant. For dessert, there is an irresistible selection of baklava, both traditional and contemporary, as well as custards and a delectable rendering of apricots in light cream. $$½ ♥

★★½ **MALABAR**—1426 Third Avenue (at 81st Street)—472-4500—In French slang, Malabar means "tough guy." But with the exception of an ornamental antelope skull hanging on a far wall, there's nothing sinister about this smartly decorated new spot. Fried goat cheese fritters with chunky tomato and cumin salsa, "red bliss" potato chips with guacamole (better ordered as an extra vegetable with dinner rather than as a first course), grilled paillard of salmon, individual focaccia pizza. Malabar also offers a short "kid's menu" of "dinosaur" pasta with marinara sauce, and fried chicken. Very enthusiastic staff. $$½ 🍷🍷

★★½ **DIVINO**—1556 Second Avenue (near 81st Street)—861-1096—Not just another Upper East Side Italian restaurant. In fact, the food here has broken free from Italian-American clichés and, if you go with the owner's suggestions, you'll dine very well indeed and there are good wines to be had for under $30 a bottle. Sautéed wild mushrooms, sausage and artichokes, veal chop, cotechino with lentils, capellini with broccoli di rape, ravioli ricotto, chicken romano. Be sure to ask for the paprika flavored bread steaks. $$$$½ 🍷🍷🍷

★★★★ **MAZZEI**—1564 Second Avenue (near 81st Street)—628-3131—Named after an 18th century Italian-American patriot, Mazzei is very much the master of contemporary kitchen diplomacy. This smallish trattoria has taken off over the course of the year, and it is now imperative to book well in advance. There's a concise, but carefully conceived menu, with nightly specials from the wood burning oven, plus excellent focaccio and bread sticks. Baked bocconcini wrapped in prosciutto, sautéed calamari in a tomato sauce, grilled mushrooms, gnocchi in a wild mushroom sauce, superb Cornish hen with peperoncini, skate with fresh peppers, and scallops with peas. Spectacular zabaglione. The premises are warm and comfortable—definitely the setting for some first-rate dining. $$$ 🍷🍷

★★½ **MARCELLO**—1568 First Avenue (near 81st Street)—628-6565—The ebullient and dedicated Marcello Silii (who had a restaurant of the same name some years ago) has taken over the former premises of Dieci (in which he once had equity) and continues to produce Italian food that is neither trendy nor particularly imaginative, but he does a good job, and his ingredients are first rate, especially his mozzarella, veal, and fresh pastas. $$$$ ♛♛♛

★★½ **GIRASOLE**—151 East 82nd Street (between Lexington and Third Avenues)—772-6690—A pleasing pastel interior that lacks soundproofing can result in almost more clamor than it's worth. The kitchen's output more than helps to compensate. Sardinian pasta with sage and wild mushrooms, broccoli di rape with sausage, veal chop Milanese. Good ricotta cheesecake. $$$$ ♛♛

★★★ **LE REFUGE**—166 East 82nd Street (between Third and Lexington Avenues)—861-4505—A charming Upper East Side bistro lodged in a townhouse. Though the decor is sparse, the bourgeois cooking more than compensates. Inspired appetizers and specials. Good supreme de volaille, medallions of veal, calf's liver. $$$ ♛♛♛

★★ **MAMBO GRILL**—174 East 82nd Street (between Third and Lexington Avenues—879-5516—An unexpected and welcome neighborhood arrival serving an appetizing array of Venezuelan specialties in surroundings best described as semi-tropical smart. For appetizers, consider ceviche of scallops or arepas rellenas (stuffed cornmeal cakes) with succulent fillings ranging from roast pork and hot sauce to black beans and white cheese. Shredded flank steak with rice, black beans, and fried plantains, sautéed shrimps with tomato, sweet chiles and saffron sauce, griddle platters, vegetarian plate. Live music Wednesday night. Lunch Saturday and Sunday only. $$½ ♛♛

★★ **OUR PLACE**—1444 Third Avenue (corner 82nd Street)—288-4888—Presided over by the former chef of Fu's, Our Place proffers a pleasing array of dishes —both Cantonese and Szechuan. Fried shrimp balls, Szechuan peppery chicken, tangerine beef, grilled and sautéed rack of lamb, Buddha's delight (medley of fresh vegetables). $$½ ♛

★★ **CAFE METAIRIE**—1442 Third Avenue (near 82nd Street)—988-1800—A down-scaled version of La Metairie restaurant which previously occupied this space (former owner Sylvain Fareri has returned to newly expanded premises in The Village), the Cafe succeeds largely on account of its attractive interior and reasonable prices. Still vaguely Provencal in form and content, with a hearty menu that includes spinach timbale, coq au vin, and cassoulet. $$$ 🍷🍷

★★ **KOO KOO'S BISTRO**—1584 Second Avenue (at 82nd Street)—737-2322—A smart-looking neighborhood place, peppered with vintage advertisements, which offers an eclectic range of bistro fare. Good fried calamari, country paté, steak frites, crabcakes, calf's liver with orange, double chocolate cake. Nice wine list. Amex only. $$½ 🍷

★★ **PRIMAVERA**—1578 First Avenue (at 82nd Street)—861-8608—Crowds still flock to this darkly-paneled, clubby establishment, even though the fare can be wildly inconsistent. Some signature dishes like roasted goat can dazzle, but on a recent visit the monkfish was sub-standard and even the pasta aioli paled. Extensive but expensive wine list. Dinner only. $$$$ 🍷🍷🍷

★★½ **ERMINIA**—250 East 83rd Street (near Third Avenue)—879-4284—A warm interior and sense of romance greet you at this cozy trattoria (sister to Trastevere). The menu has been updated of late, so along with excellent pasta specials and grilled fare or staples like veal pizzaiolo, you'll find additions like swordfish rollatine, with pine nuts and raisins. $$$ 🍷🍷

★ **THE POLO GROUNDS**—1472 Third Avenue (near 83th Street)—570-5590—If you've ever been torn between canceling your dinner reservation or leaving your favorite team in the lurch as they play into overtime on T.V., this one's for you: Oversized television screens and regular sets tuned to the evening's prime sports event are the key attraction at this casual spot, where salads, light pastas and burgers play second fiddle. Cover charge on occasion. $$ 🍷

★★ **MOCCA HUNGARIAN RESTAURANT**—1588 Second Avenue (near 83rd Street)—734-6470—If you are feeling low and want to experience a little sentimental reverie of New York, head straight for Mocca Hungarian, where you'll find some well made, though not particularly refined Hungarian specialties like gulyas and chicken paprikas and dessert crêpes.

Drink the robust red Hungarian wine, Egri Bikaver, and you'll feel very happy within a few moments. No credit cards. $$½ ♟

★½ **ALBERO D'ORO**—1589 Second Avenue (near 83rd Street)—517-4448—Reservations can be problematic here. On our last recent visit, our confirmed table required over half an hour's wait. And if only the meal had concluded with the glorious antipasti—bruschetta, pizzette, and assorted caponata and carciofi, the inconvenience would have been forgotten. But the pasta simply didn't aspire to the same heights, and the mixed grill disappointed. Calamari Albera D'Oro recommended. Tiramisu. Amex only. $$$½ ♟♟

★★★½ **VICO RISTORANTE**—1603 Second Avenue (near 83rd Street)—772-7441—An intimate, white-walled, sliver of a space that has become an instant hit (and spawned two equally popular outposts, Sette Mezzo and Vico Madison, q.v.) Bordering on boisterous, this neighborhood trattoria more than offsets the noise-level with wonderful home-spun pastas and innovative creations such as wilted arugula with grilled smoked mozzarella, expertly fried zucchini, and baby artichokes, country sausage with broccoli, flattened breaded veal chop with pecans, tiramisu. Dinner only. No credit cards. $$½ ♟♟

★★ **TRASTEVERE**—309 East 83rd Street (near Second Avenue)—734-6343—The original country-Italian trattoria out of three spawned siblings. Cramped and high in decibels, the place is something of a victim of its success and you can wait forever. Spiedino alla romana, cappellini, tartufo. Dinner only. $$$ ♟♟

★★★ **TRIANGOLO**—345 East 83rd Street (between First and Second Avenues)—472-4488—A charming trattoria (striped yellow awnings give it a very fresh look) that escapes the traditional mold. Very good pasta with duck ragout, calamari with balsamic vinegar, pork chops pizzaiolo, scallopine of veal with tomatoes, mozzarella and capers, gelati. No credit cards. $$$ ♟♟♟

★★ **WILKINSON'S SEAFOOD CAFE**—1573 York

Avenue (near 83rd Street)—535-5454—A welcome addition to an area distinguished only by its multitude of fast-food outlets. A friendly decor is the setting for accomplished, though slightly routine seafood preparations. Good crabeat gallette, seafood sausage, shrimp with teriyaki-ginger glaze, grilled swordfish, and white chocolate mousse. $$ ☖

★½ **NICOLA'S**—146 East 84th Street (near Lexington Avenue)—249-9850—In the swinging 70s when Nick (a former captain at Elaine's q.v.) presided over this raffish trattoria, this was a place to see and be seen. Although Nick is now gone, and the premises have been given a complete face-lift, (some say for the worse) the place remains a popular, if not self-possessed Upper East Side hangout—good for pastas, and simple grilled fare. $$$ ☖

★★★ **ELIO'S**—1621 Second Avenue (at 84th Street)—772-2242—Festive, though noisy Upper East Side hangout patronized by its fair share of celebs. Very dependable pasta preparations, good calamari and veal chops. Good selection of wines. Dinner only. $$$½ ☖

★★ **BISTRO BAMBOCHE**—1582 York Avenue (near 84th Street)—249-4002—A small and intimate interior, with exposed brick walls, serving up continental bistro fare with a few unusual Eastern European borrowings like pickel soup. Otherwise, expect decent broiled scallops with burnt butter sauce, veal chop, steak au poivre. $$½ ☖

★½ **AL BACIO**—245 East 84th Street (near Second Avenue)—744-9343—Management has made much of the homestyle Italian cooking here based on Mama's sacred recipes, but we found nothing to enrapture us and much to criticize, like gummy cheese on the pizzette, disastrous risotto with mushrooms, and dreary zuppa di pesce. The premises are a bit glitzy, the service staff needs experience, and the dessert maker needs lessons. Dinner only. $$$$ ☖

★★★ **AZZURRO**—1625 Second Avenue (near 84th Street)—517-7068—Pretty close to the ideal Italian trattoria, and one of the first, five years ago, to spur interest in regional Italian cookery, in this case Sicilian. A lot of other, pricier places have disappeared, but Azzurro, with its tiny dining room simply decorated with blue ceiling, Renaissance prints and marionettes, is turning out food that's better than ever, and service, once perfunctory, is now very courteous. Prices are very fair for food of an extremely tasty, robust variety. Caponata, bucatini with sardines and fennel sauce, sautéed spinach and garlic, chicken with sausage, involtini of veal. $$$½ ☕☕

★★★ **PAOLA'S RESTAURANT**—347 East 85th Street (near First Avenue)—794-1890—Tiny, tinceilinged trattoria packed with traditional, old-world charm. Excellent crostini, sautéed Jerusalem artichokes, ravioli with ricotta and basil, pasta with red snapper, lamb stew, chicken with sausage, tiramisu. $$½ ☕☕

☺● **ELAINE'S**—1703 Second Avenue (near 88th Street)—534-8103—A truly awful great place. It may still reign supreme as a literary/celebrity hang-out for the likes of Woody Allen, Gay Talese, and David Halberstam, and owner Elaine Kauffman makes her chums feel coddled. But the food is nowhere near as stellar as the clientele, the place looks like its needs a good scrubbing, and the waiters think they're doing you a favor by admitting you. Our last meal consisted of tasteless eggplant rollatine, gummy gnocchi, insipid capellini with sliced mushrooms, but a first-rate veal chop. $$$½ ☕

★★★ **TABLE D'HOTE**—44 East 92nd Street (between Madison and Park Avenues)—348-8125—Despite its small size (virtually a hole in the wall with only a handful of tables), Table D'Hote serves up first rate fare in a most attractive, antique filled surrounding. Each place setting displays a different set of china. Snails in puff pastry, goat cheese croquettes, black bean soup with jalapeño cream, grilled chicken breast with wild rice and cabbage, grilled salmon, baby lamb, tarte Tatin. Nice assortment of wines by the glass. $$$ ☕☕☕

★½ **BUSBY'S**—45 East 92nd Street (off Madison)—360-7373—A new addition to upper Madison's restaurant row, specializing in grilled fare—chicken, fish and beef—along with a few ambitious entrees—sweet and sour calamari, swordfish stuffed with mozzarella and sun-dried tomatoes. $$$ 🍷

★½ **CAFFE EQUENSE**—1291 Madison Avenue (near 91st Street)—860-2300—A pleasant neighborhood spot with a haunting Hopperesque mural and a fairly standard Italian menu you'll find up and down the East Side. The pizzas are of some interest, but the calamari were rubbery, the grilled eggplant and zucchini served ice cold, and the desserts were below average. $$$ 🍷

★★ **SARABETH'S KITCHEN**—1295 Madison Avenue (near 92nd Street)—410-7335—A cozy spot, redolent of a tea room, noted for its baked goods. You can also count on delectable omlettes, frittatas, pasta and oversized sandwiches, plus seafood specials. No reservations. $½ 🍷

★★★ **VICO MADISON**—1302 Madison Avenue (between 92nd and 93rd Streets)—876-2222—With a roomy and attractive modern interior, and a menu similar to its successful siblings, Vico on Second Avenue and Sette Mezzo on Lexington Avenue (q.v.), it is no surprise that Vico Madison has become an instant hit with the Carnegie Hill set. You can count on pleasing lunchtime salads, stuffed or grilled mozzarela, pasta specials and signature dishes like breaded veal chop with pecans. No credit cards. $$½ 🍷

★★½ **ISLAND**—1305 Madison Avenue (between 92nd and 93rd Streets)—996-1200—An extremely affable little Riviera-style restaurant with a lot of Preppies in evidence. Bistro chairs, bellinis served by the pitcher, and lovely, sunny food. Can be a little rushed and noisy, but the menu more than compensates. Savory tarts, swordfish with cream of arugala, grilled rabbit, tarte tatin. $$$ 🍷

★★★ **BISTRO DU NORD**—1312 Madison Avenue (near 93rd Street) —289-0997—A delightful sliver of a space stacked two stories high and chock a block with vintage photos by the likes of Atget, Avedon and Irving Penn. A sedate neighborhood luncheon spot, this bistro bristles at night with a cosmopolitan crowd that descends from all over. Good salads and patés, steak marchand de vin, grilled salmon with warm vinaigrette. Pleasant wine list. $$$½ ⚇

★★ **SARANAC**—1350 Madison Avenue (near 95th Street)—289-9600—Kitchy Adirondack decor—water-side murals, mounted antlers, carved booths—redeems what otherwise would be described as a contemporary cafeteria. An eclectic menu should accommodate most tastes—such basics as burgers and french fries, light salads and aged sirloin steak, to more elaborate preparations like shrimp bisque, fried calamari, and Chesapeake soft shell crab sandwich. Good key lime pie. No reservations. Amex only. $$½ ⚇

SIXTY-SIXTH STREET TO HARLEM (WEST)

○ ★★★½ **CAFE DES ARTISTES**—1 West 67th Street (near Central Park West)—877-3500—The history surrounding Café des Artistes dates to just after World War I when the apartment building here was home to many of the era's finest artists, none more famous than Howard Chandler Christy, who painted the celebrated murals of naked nymphs romping in what looks like Central Park. The beautiful dining room is made for romance, and owner George Lang demands high standards. This is a perfect place before or after Lincoln Center. Expect to see some of the city's most notable notables dining here. Pot au feu, chicken pot pie, cassoulet, Ilona Torte. $$$$ ⚇⚇⚇

○ ★★★ **TAVERN ON THE GREEN**—67th Street and Central Park West—873-3200—Everyone's heard of this fanciful restaurant and people come here to bask in the flamboyance of Warner LeRoy's Central Park fantasy of lights and antique kitsch that overwhelms and seduces. Yes, it's an "out-of-towners'" restaurant, yes, it's the big banquet place, but the food in the main dining room, under chef Marc Poidevin (formerly of Maxim's), is very good indeed, with specials

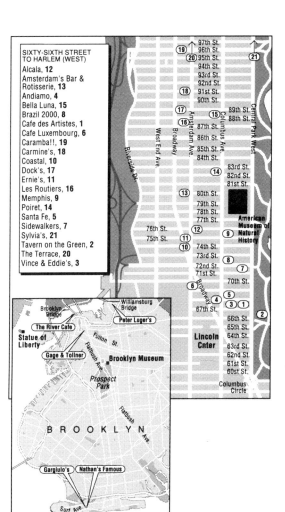

SIXTY-SIXTH STREET
TO HARLEM (WEST)
Alcala, **12**
Amsterdam's Bar &
Rotisserie, **13**
Andiamo, **4**
Bella Luna, **15**
Brazil 2000, **8**
Cafe des Artistes, **1**
Cafe Luxembourg, **6**
Caramba!!, **19**
Carmine's, **18**
Coastal, **10**
Dock's, **17**
Ernie's, **11**
Les Routiers, **16**
Memphis, **9**
Poiret, **14**
Santa Fe, **5**
Sidewalkers, **7**
Sylvia's, **21**
Tavern on the Green, **2**
The Terrace, **20**
Vince & Eddie's, **3**

like red snapper with fried leeks and shiitakes in a red wine sauce and quail risotto as stand-out dishes. So are all the desserts, like a waffle with poached pears and praline ice cream. The French fries are unsurpassed, the hamburger still one of the best. The pre-theater menu, from $19.50–$23.50, is an amazing bargain. $$$$½ ☵☵☵

★★★ **VINCE & EDDIE'S**—70 West 68th Street (between Central Park West and Columbus Avenue)—721-0068—Named after owners Vincent Orgera (who tends bar) and Eddie Schoenfeld, former maitre d'/impresario at Auntie Yuan's and Shun Lee, this place hasn't looked back since its successful debut last year. The attractive, modified country look was orchestrated by Sam Lopata. The menu is devoid of gimmickry; it simply works well and costs less. Onion tart, fried oysters, calf's liver with apples and onion rings, lamb shank, mashed turnip with crisped shallots, red snapper with walnuts, apple tureen. Garden dining in season. Beware of over-booking. $$$ ☵☵

★★½ **ANDIAMO**—1991 Broadway (near 68th Street, but you actually enter via an altogether separate courtyard café)—362-3315—A strikingly contemporary interior—very high tech, replete with new wave paintings and sculpture. Andiamo serves up an enticing and eclectic array of specialties. Roasted sweet red peppers and mozzarella, angel hair pasta with seafood in a saffron broth, grilled lamb chop with couscous. No smoking throughout. Closed Monday. $$$½ ☵☵☵

★★ **SANTA FE**—72 West 69th Street (near Columbus Avenue)—724-0822—Part of the first wave of trendy Manhattan Tex-Mex eateries, and still going strong. The peach interior is warm and inviting, and the menu is comforting but somewhat jaded. Tacos al carbon. $$ ☵

★★★ **CAFE LUXEMBOURG**—200 West 70th Street (near Amsterdam Avenue)—873-7411—Now verging on institutional status, this is a relatively informal and still very stylish outpost for late night dining on the Upper West Side. Bistro fare can be quite creative here. Potato and fennel vichyssoise, steak frites, baby lamb, profiteroles with white chocolate mint chip ice cream. $$$ ♛♛♛

★★ **SIDEWALKERS**—12 West 72nd Street (near Central Park West)—799-6070—NYC's only Maryland crab house, where you pound and pick away at spiced blue crabs and drink beer. The huge dining room, which appears to once have been a lobby, is jammed with casually dressed West Siders. Creole gumbo excellent but rest of the dishes not up to those crabs. $$$ ♛

★★ **BRAZIL 2000**—127 West 72nd Street—(near Columbus Avenue)—877-7730—Though the decor lacks sparkle, there's nothing to fault on the menu at this reasonably priced Brazilian eatery. The sinfully delicious caipirinhas (sugar-cane rum, lemon juice and sugar) will conjure up all the Brazilian revelry that's missing. Add the aperitivos Brasileiros, linguicafrita and churrasco gaucho, and the effect is complete. $$½ ♛

★ **COASTAL**—300 Amsterdam Avenue (near 74th Street)—769-3988—Boisterous and loud, this nondescript Upper West Side seafood restaurant has little to recommend it—especially the food, which is at best pretty fair, like the soft shell crabs in brown butter, and the blueberry pie. No place for a serious meal. $$$ ♛

★ **ERNIE'S**—2150 Broadway (near 75th Street)—496-1588—Enormous brick space decorated in the International style. Friendly neighborhood atmosphere, noisy, crowded bar. Pizzas and pastas still popular. $$ ♛

★★ **MEMPHIS**—329 Columbus Avenue (between 75th and 76th Street)—496-1840—Striking, two-tiered eatery with Corinthian columns marrying high-tech exotica with down-home, mostly Cajun American cooking. Results are uneven, decibel level outrageous, bar jammed with singles—a great crowd pleaser nonetheless. Warm goat cheese and fried chicken salad, Cajun popcorn, crab pancake, Southern fried chicken with mashed potatoes, jambalaya. Dinner only. $$$ ♛♛♛

★★ **ALCALA**—349 Amsterdam Avenue—(near 76th Street)—769-9600—An innovative Spanish restaurant cum tapas bar, designed for conservative uptown tastes. The decor is unassuming (the ubiquitous brick and brass look) and at times, the food can be equally restrained. Good tapas, such as empañadas and wild mushrooms with chorizo, mussels in salsa verde. Seafood paella can be garlicky; try the chicken and rabbit paella with sausages instead. Decent wine list. Open 7 days a week. $$$ ⚇

★★ **AMSTERDAM'S BAR AND ROTISSERIE**—428 Amsterdam Avenue (near 80th Street)—874-1377—This fast became a popular Upper West Side hangout, and jockeying for tables here was elevated to an art form. Its popularity is well deserved, not just because the prices are downright low and the portions enormous, but the food is very good and you'll have a real sense of what the West Side is all about. Roast chicken, steaks, French fries, dessert pies. $$ ⚇

★★½ **POIRET**—474 Columbus Avenue (between 82nd and 83rd Street)—724-6880—White walls with a floral motif, candle-lit tables, and a flower-festooned vitrine create an instantly airy ambience at this popular French eaterie. The only flaw is the sound proofing. But the first-rate bistro fare more than compensates, even when you have to raise your voice a tad to be heard over the beautifully seasoned and flavorful Mediterranean soup. Chicken-liver mousse and frisé salad delight. Whether you order the steak au poivre or steak béarnaise, be sure to request a side dish of frites. For dessert, an admirable crème brûlée. Dinner only. $$$ ⚇⚇⚇

★★ **LES ROUTIERS**—568 Amsterdam Avenue—(between 87th and 88th Streets)—874-2742—A simple looking bistro that bills itself as "a taste of the French countryside in Manhattan." In its pleasant bouillabaisse, charcuterie, riesling-flavored choucroute garni, steak au poivre and crepe banane, it accomplishes just that. Very reasonable wine list. Dinner only. $$½ ⚇⚇

★★ **BELLA LUNA**—584 Columbus Avenue (between 88th and 89th Streets)—877-2267—A cheery, contemporary spot for simple pastas and grilled fare. The place is casual, and the pace is lively. Herb marinated shrimp, fried calamari, grilled chicken with arugula salad, seared sliced beef. No credit cards. $$½ 🍷

★★½ **DOCK'S**—2427 Broadway, (near 89th Street)—724-5588—This is a highly popular spot for seafood, contemporary in look but with the charm of an old-time seafood house. You dine on two separate levels separated by stairs and a gleaming brass rail. A blackboard lists the daily oyster specials, along with the catch of the day (which will also be rhymed off by your waiter.) Such staples as Caesar salad, grilled scallops, salmon and grilled halibut. $$$ 🍷🍷

★★ **CARMINE'S**—2450 Broadway (near 91st Street)—362-2200—Those who wouldn't deign to set foot in Little Italy or have never eaten in the Bronx, Brooklyn or Queens, have made Carmine's a retro-chic restaurant of daunting popularity—a big, sprawling, loud, red-sauce, family place with old-fashioned Italian-American food served in double portions at very fair prices. Not that Carmine's is any better than dozens of other Italian-American restaurants in NYC; it has just caught on and people wait an hour or more in a smoke-engulfed bar to gorge here on rubbery calamari, very good pastas, and nice, garlicky chicken scarpariello. Volume business means volume cooking and slow service. $$½ 🍷

★ **CARAMBA!!**—2567 Broadway (at 96th Street)—749-5055—One of the loudest spots in NYC serving some pretty humdrum, sometimes greasy Tex-Mex food. The chili can be terrific. The staff is dressed in company t-shirts and is none too swift in getting orders right. If you're dying for some nachos (which are very good), truck on over. There are outposts of Caramba!! also at 1576 Third Avenue, 918 Eighth Avenue, and 684 Broadway. $$½ 🍷

★★★★ **THE TERRACE**—400 West 119th Street (near Amsterdam Avenue)—666-9490—Perched atop a Columbia University dorm (though not associated with the school), this elegant dining room, with its panoramic view of Manhattan and the Hudson River, is packed most nights but unfamiliar to many New Yorkers. The food is every bit the equal of the view, with prices just about comparable to downtown deluxe. Chef Ossama Mickail presides over the kitchen and delivers the likes of quail with caramelized squash, red snapper with coriander and tomato confit, mint chocolate ice cream profiteroles. Service is most professional. $48 fixed price and à la carte. $$$$$ ♀♀♀

★★½ **SYLVIA'S**—329 Lenox Avenue (near 126th Street)—996-0660—If you're craving great barbecue, downhome soul food, and something uniquely New York, catch a cab up to Harlem to Sylvia's, a marvelous restaurant serving up batches of great ribs, pork chops, candied sweet potatoes, and pecan pies that will satisfy the biggest eater in family. It is true that the neighborhood is not exactly inviting, but once inside, you'll be treated royally. No credit cards. $$½ ♀

BEYOND MANHATTAN
BROOKLYN

★★ **GAGE & TOLLNER**—372 Fulton Street (on Fulton Mall)—718-875-5181—On looks alone, this 112 year old landmark restaurant warrants a visit. Authentic gas lamps, (among the last remaining examples in the city), roomy banquettes and an old fashioned layout create a charming, old New York feel. But despite the initial uplift provided by Edna Lewis's cooking, the food has been inconsistent of late, and service can be erratic. On a good day, signature appetizers worth sampling include Charleston she-crab soup, crab cakes and lobster bisque. As an alternative, there are dozens of clam and oyster starters, like soft clam belly fritters. Shrimp and crab gumbo, crab cakes Freetown, braised brisket of beef and corn fritters are worth a try. $$$½ ♀♀

○ ★★★½ **THE RIVER CAFE**—1 Water Street (under the Brooklyn Bridge)—718-522-5200—The extraordinary view of the East River, the Brooklyn Bridge, and the Manhattan cityscape, make this a must-go for a unique sense of New York's majesty. Chef David Burke displays real talent, and while his food is still highly stylized, he appears to have tamed his more eccentric tendencies. Sautéed sea scallops with fennel seed, prawn falafels, barbecued squab with foie gras and corn cake, salmon with ginger, yellowfin tuna with asparagus and prosciutto, filet of beef with noolde cake, apple tart, Napoleon of bittersweet chocolate crunch. The dining room has no bad tables, but to secure one of the coveted seats by the window you'll have to "negotiate" with the maitre d'. Brunch is a wonderful time to go, but book far in advance. Fixed price $58. Tasting menu $75. ♥♥♥♥

★★½ **PETER LUGER**—178 Broadway—718-387-7400—There's no question that Peter Luger is a bit of 19th-century New York that deserves veneration. The Teutonic look, once common in chophouses, has its charm, and so do the deliberately brusque waiters. You have little choice in ordering—a nondescript tomato and onion salad, sensational Porterhouse (prepared for two or more people), very good lamb chops, okay hash browns, bland creamed spinach, and the usual cheesecake. Worth a journey through some pretty rough territory? (An attendant will watch your car.) Perhaps out of homage, or as a novelty for an out-of-towner. But the food's as good —and far more varied—at The Palm, Smith & Wollensky, and Spark's in Manhattan. $$$$½ ♥

★★ **GARGIULO'S**—2911 West 15th Street (near Surf Avenue)—718-266-4891—If you find yourself at Coney Island, have a frank at Nathan's or visit this sprawling Southern Italian restaurant with its garish decor, friendly waiters, and large portions of spicy food. Good buy. $$$ ♥♥

★★ **NATHAN'S FAMOUS**—1315 Surf Avenue (at Stillwell Avenue)—718-946-2202—This is a grand institution, as old as the Brooklyn Dodgers but obviously more durable. Nathan Handwerker didn't invent the hot dog, but he did more to popularize it than anyone else, and it's still a nonpareil frank. The Coney Island location has nostalgia on its side; the Times Square branch does not. $

THE BRONX

★★★★★ **AMERIGO'S**—3587 East Tremont Avenue (near the Long Island Sound)—792-3600—A Throgs Neck (safe neighborhood) institution for half a century, Amerigo's, under owners Tony and Anna Cortese, gets better every year. There are two dining rooms, one casual, the other a bit more refined, with low lighting, Italianate sculpture, and a spacious bar. The osso buco is the best in NYC, the pastas all superb, the pork chops with vinegar peppers sublime, and the steaks rich and beefy. Prices for enormous portions are very fair and the mostly Italian wine list very comprehensive. Closed Mondays. $$$½ ♛♛♛♛

★ **DOMINICK'S**—2335 Arthur Avenue (3 blocks from Fordham Road)—733-2807—We wouldn't even bother listing Dominick's except that so many people think it's some gem in the wilderness and that it's worth waiting on a line to get in, sitting at communal tables, having so-so Italian-American food literally dropped in front of you, having no wine list from which to choose and being told by the waiter at his whim what this is all going to cost you. Dominick's is a silly joke and bears no resemblance to what good Italian cooking or hospitality should be. Go across the street to Mario's and you'll be struck by the difference. Closed Tuesday. $$$ ♛

★★★ **MARIO'S**—2342 Arthur Avenue (near Fordham Road)—584-1188—Arthur Avenue is a marvelous Italian market street and Mario's is where everybody eats. Here since 1919 and a second home to the NY Yankees, it is a good Neapolitan restaurant with zesty, freshly made food and some of the best pizzas you'll ever eat. Ask for Mama Miglucci's hot pepper carrots. Cavatelli al filetto di pomodoro, stuffed eggplant, octopus salad. Closed Monday. $$½ ♛

WESTCHESTER

★★★½ **BUFFET DE LA GARE**—155 Southside Avenue, Hastings-on-Hudson, NY—914-478-1671—Devoted owners Gwanael and Annie Goulet run this charming (recently expanded) little dining room on the Hudson with great panache and love. Known for its robust bistro fare like cassoulet and boeuf a la bourguignonne, Gwanael has also gained a reputation for dishes of subtlety and refinement, from halibut with red peppers and galette of potatoes, sautéd foie gras and profiteroles. About 45 minutes from NYC. Closed Sundays and Mondays. $$$½ ♈♈♈

★★★ **PINOCCHIO**—309 White Plains Road, Eastchester—914-337-0044—Were Pinocchio in Manhattan it would be judged one of the better Italian restaurants. The dining room is sedate, unencumbered and casual, but the kitchen really sparkles with flavors and seasonings. The service staff on weekends is very overworked and delays can be frustrating. Polenta with four cheeses, penne alla arrabbiata, chicken riviera. $$$½ ♈

★★★★★ **MAXIME'S**—Old Tomahawk Road, Granite Springs, NY—914-248-7200—Maxime Ribera, who established his reputation years ago at NYC's Café Argenteuil, almost singlehandedly sparked the movement for grand cuisine in the NY area suburbs. Here, in a beautifully furnished dining room with fireplace and fine art, Maxime and his wife Hugette run a paragon of a French restaurant. The food is of the very highest quality, ranking with the best in the USA. The wine list is unassailable. This is well worth the one hour trip from Manhattan. Trout with fennel cream, roast pigeon with cabbage, all venison dishes, chocolate terrine. Closed Monday. Fixed price: $52. ♈♈♈♈

★★★★ **AUBERGE MAXIME**—Route 116, North Salem, NY—914-669-5450—Charming, isolated (it's about an hour from NYC) and very, very romantic, Auberge Maxime has for years been a favorite in this region, and on any given night the parking lot is jammed. The woods surround the property and both the upstairs and the new downstairs dining rooms are as cozy and cheery as owners Bernard and Heidi LeBris can make them. Bernard is as good at making classic confits and duck a la presse as he is novel dishes like smoked scallops and shrimp and grilled crisp salmon. The wine list is excellent, especially strong in French offerings. Closed Wednesday. Fixed price: $47; also a la carte. $$$$

★★★★½ **LA PANETIERE**—530 Milton Road, Rye—914-967-8140—Very close in image and spirit to a restaurant in the French countryside, La Panetiere epitomizes the very finest traditions of service and dedication to high ideals. Owner Jacques Loupiac is committed to making this one of the best restaurants and wine cellars in the US, and chef Thomas Henkelmann, formerly of NYC's Maurice and before that the renowned Auberge de L'Ille in Alsace, has given the kitchen a new direction. Shellfish saffron couscous, veal shank, sweetbreads, and filet with endives, napoleon of crepes with orange. Jackets required. Fixed price $48 (4 courses) and $65 (6 courses).

★★★½ **HUNAN VILLAGE**—1828 Central Park Avenue, Yonkers—914-779-2272—Bright, friendly and overseen by the indefatigable Paul Chou, this has some of the best Chinese cooking in the region, but you should always ask Paul to guide you to the specials. Clams in black bean sauce, potted chicken with ginger and wine, Village prawn with broccoli, filet of sole with butter sauce and bok choy. $$

★★★ **LA CREMAILLERE**—Banksville, NY—914-234-9647—With its timbered decor, provençal murals, and fine china, this is the ideal country French restaurant. The menu is still quite classic but growing in scope, and the desserts are quite spectacular. The wine list is superb. Prices are very expensive here, however, easily as much as you'll pay in Manhattan. Lobster and crab salad, chicken veuve brush, halibut with basil sauce, raspberry crème brûlée. Closed Monday. $$$$$

CONNECTICUT

★★★ **LA GRANGE AT THE HOMESTEAD INN**—420 Field Point Road, Greenwich,—203-869-7500—A finely restored farmhouse on rolling fields is the setting for what is certainly one of the most idyllic country inns in New England. The rustic dining room, designed by John Saladino, is impeccable, just one example of owners Nancy Smith and Lessi Davison's dedication to their faithful clientele. Chef Jacques Thiebaud has moved beyond classic formulas and brightened up the menu some, though the sauces could still be lighter. Tomato soup, broiled red snapper with vermouth and mushrooms, pheasant with celery root, chocolate seven-layer cake. $$$$$ ♥♥♥♥

★★★★½ **RESTAURANT JEAN-LOUIS**—61 Lewis Street, Greenwich—203-622-8450—Jean-Louis Gérin is one of those indefatigable, endlessly inventive chefs who runs a very personalized little dining room. His wife Linda greets you, and the staff is well trained to explain Gérin's dishes. The small dining room is bright, pretty, and mirrored, and enjoys a very steady, knowledgeable clientele from the surrounding area and Manhattan. Sautéed lobster with arugala and thyme, sweetbreads and saffron tea, soft shell crabs with garlic and lemon, sliced venison and juniper butter. Closed Sunday. $$$$$ ♥♥♥♥

★★★½ **BERTRAND**—253 Greenwich Avenue, Greenwich CT—203-661-4459—Christian Bertrand, for more than a decade sous-chef to André Soltner at NYC's Lutece (q.v.), opened his own place two years ago quickly established himself as a contender among the first-rate chefs in the Tri-State region. The three-level dining room is striking, with tiled arched ceilings and tall windows, and the service staff is impeccably trained. Rillettes of duck on brioche, sweetbreads with veal filet on spinach and fried celery, apple tart, succes cake. Very good wine list, with some buys in Burgundy. $$$$½ ♥♥♥

FOOD DICTIONARY

FRENCH

Aiguillettes de canard—duck breasts
Aïoli—a garlic mayonnaise
Ananas—pineapple
Béchamel—a white, milk-based sauce
Beurre blanc—"white butter" sauce
Beurre noir—"black butter," a cooked brown butter sauce
Boeuf à la bourguignonne—beef stew cooked in red wine
Bordelaise—a demiglace and red wine sauce with parsley and
    shallots
Bouillabaisse—Marseilles seafood stew
Bourride—provençal fish stew with garlic mayonnaise
Brandade de morue—pureed cod, garlic and potatoes
Cassis—black currant
Cassoulet—dish of beans, pork, preserved duck, sausage and
    seasonings
Cerise—cherry
Chanterelle—wild mushroom shaped like small trumpet
Chantilly—served with lightly whipped cream
Chevreuil—venison
Choucroute garni—smoked pork, sausage, preserved duck and
    sauerkraut
Civet—stew
Citron—lemon
Confit de canard—duck meat preserved in its own fat
Confiture—a jam-like reduction of fruit or vegetables
Crème à l'anglaise—a thickened custard sauce
Crème brûlée—dessert custard with a burned sugar crust
Daube—braised meat
Dijonnaise—mustard sauce
Duxelles—minced mushrooms
Écrevisse—crayfish
En gelée—in jellied aspic
Espadon—swordfish
Faisan—pheasant
Farci—stuffed
Financière—with mushrooms, Madeira and truffles
Forestière—cooked with mushrooms
Fraîche—fresh
Frisée—curly leaf lettuce
Fruits de mer—seafood
Galette—a small cake
Grand veneur—"hunter style," with red wine, cream and
    currant jelly
Grillade—grilled meat
Ile flottante—"Floating island" meringues in custard

Italienne—demiglace flavored with tomato and bacon
Langoustine—large shrimp
Lapin—rabbit
Lardon—bacon
Lentilles—lentils
Mâche—lamb's lettuce
Maïs—corn
Marjolaine—a richly textured chocolate and hazelnut cake
Mesclun—mixed wildgreens
Meunière—fish cooked in butter and lemon
Mille-feuille—puff pastry
Morille—wild mushroom, morel
Mornay—béchamel sauce enriched with cheese
Moules—mussels
Navarin—lamb stew
Nouilles—noodles
Oursin—sea urchin
Pâté—forcemeat cut in slabs
Pâte—pastry
Périgourdine—demiglace sauce with truffles
Pied-de-porc—pig's feet
Pintadeau—guinea hen
Poireaux—leeks
Poivre vert—green pepper
Pommes—apples
Poularde—large roasting chicken
Poussin—young chicken
Praline—caramelized, pulverized almonds
Raie—skate
Ravigote—vinegar-based caper, onion and herbs sauce
Rémoulade—mayo flavored with mustard and gherkins and
    anchovy essence
Rillettes—pork or goose mashed with fat
Ris de veau—veal sweetbreads
Rognon—kidney
Rouget—red mullet
Saint-Pierre—John Dory fish
Suprême de volaille—boneless breast of chicken, sautéed in butter
Tarte Tatin—hot apple tart
Thon—tuna
Tripes à la mode de Caen—tripe cooked in an onion, bacon and
    garlic sauce
Vacherin—meringue dessert with ice cream layers
Vol-au-vent—flaky pastry shell

GREEK

Armi—lamb
Baklava—sweet flakey phyllo pastry

Dolma—stuffed grape leaves
Hummos—creamy chick pea and tahini puree
Keftedhes—seasoned meatballs
Mezze—appetizer
Psomi—bread
Taramasalata—appetizer dip of mashed cod roe

INDIAN

Aloo chat—potatoes cooked with spices
Biryani—fragrant rice dishes
Dal—lentil-based side dish
Dosa—a stuffed crepe
Gobhi—cabbage or cauliflower
Gosht do piaz—meat and onion stew
Jalebi—swirls of deep-fried batter in sugar syrup
Keema—ground meat dish
Kheer—rice cooked in milk
Kofta—meatballs
Korma—braised meat and yogurt dishes
Kulfi—ice cream with nuts
Matar paneer—spicy side dish of cheese and vegetables
Murgh—chicken
Pakoras—deep-fried vegetable dumplings
Ras malai—cheese dessert
Shorba—soup
Vindaloo—a spicy hot lamb dish

ITALIAN

Abbachio—very young lamb
Acciuga—anchovies
Aglio e olio—garlic and oil
Amatriciana—sauce of tomatoes, hot peppers and pancetta ham
Arrabbiata—a freshly-made tomato and hot pepper pasta sauce
Baccalà—salted dried cod
Bagna cauda—anchovies, garlic and pepper in which vegetables
  are cooked or dipped
Bocconcini—balls of mozzarella or veal
Bollito misto—boiled mixed meats
Bresaola—dried beef
Brodetto—fish soup
Bruschetta—toasted Italian bread, often with garlic and tomato
Bucatini—tubular pasta
Capellini—very thin spaghetti
Caponata—a hot, spicy, eggplant and pepper marinade
Cappesante—scallops
Capro—goat
Carciòfi—artichokes
Casalinga—"homestyle" food

Cipolla—onion
Coniglio—rabbit
Costoletta—cutlet
Cotechino—large pork sausage
Cozze—mussels
Fegato—liver
Fichi—figs
Finocchio—fennel
Focaccia—puffy, pizza-like bread, often sprinkled with rosemary
Fragole—strawberries
Fritto—fried
Frutti di mare—mixed seafood
Gamberi—shrimp
Gelati—ice creams
Gnocchi—potato dumplings
Grissini—breadsticks
Lenticchie—lentils
Lepre—hare
Lumache—snails
Mascarpone—a rich butter-like cheese
Melanzana—eggplant
Orecchiette—ear-shaped pasta
Ostriche—oysters
Pappardelle—flat wide pasta, sometimes shaped like butterflies
Pesto—basil, garlic, pignoli and olive oil sauce
Pignoli—pine nuts
Piselli—peas
Polenta—cooked cornmeal
Polpo—octopus
Primavera—"springtime," refers to dishes with vegetables
Puttanesca—a robust, spicy tomato and herb sauce
Radicchio—red-leafed bitter lettuce
Ragù—meat and vegetable tomato-based sauce
Risotto—cooked rice dish with other ingredients
Sarde—sardines
Tagliarini—thin spaghetti
Tagliatelle—similar to fettuccine
Tira misu—mascarpone, espresso and lady finger's dessert
Tonno—tuna
Trippa—tripe
Vitello tonnato—cold veal in creamy tuna sauce
Vongole—clams
Zuppa inglese—sponge cake doused with liqueurs and rum

JAPANESE

Daikon—white radish
Miso—red bean paste
Nori—sheets of black seaweed

Somen—fine noodles
Tatami room—private dining room
Tonkatsu—breaded pork cutlet
Wasabi—very pungent green horseradish
Yosenabe—beef, chicken and vegetables simmered in stock with
    noodles

KOREAN

Bolgogi—marinated barbecued beef
Kalbee—marinated spareribs
Kimchee—fiery hot chili condiment
Shinsonro—meat, seafood and seaweed casserole

MEXICAN

Carne asado—Mexican pot roast
Chalupas—little pastry boats" with ground meat
Chiles rellenos—stuffed chile peppers
Mole—creamy sauce often flavored with bitter chocolate
Tamales—corn husk steamed with seasonings

RUSSIAN

Basturma—marinated barbecued beef
Blini—thin buckwheat pancakes
Borsch—beet soup
Pelmeny—Russian ravioli
Pirosch—stuffed pastries
Varenyky—dessert dumplings

SPANISH

Almejas—clams
Arroz con pollo—rice and chicken dish
Bacalao—salted dried cod
Budín—pudding
Calamar—squid
Lomo—roast pork
Mariscos—shellfish
Tapas—Spanish finger food
Zarzuela—shellfish stew

THAI

Kaeng masaman—chicken or beef curry
Mee krob—crisp-fried noodles with shrimp and egg
Nam pla—fermented fish sauce
Tom yam kong—lemon grass-chili soup

FOOD INDEX

AMERICAN
7th Regiment Mess
Acme Bar & Grill
Adam's Rib
Albuquerque Eats
All American Diner
America
American Festival
　Café
American Harvest
Amsterdam's Bar
　& Rotisserie
An American Place
Arcadia
Arizona 206
BBQ
Billy's
Bouley
Bridge Café
Brighton Grill
Busby's
Carolina
Century Café, The
Charley O's
Chefs Cuisiniers
　Club
Coach House, The
Coastal
Coastal Café
Coconut Grill
Empire Diner
Fraunces Tavern
Ginger Man, The
Grill 53
Hard Rock Café
Harvey's Chelsea
　Restaurant
Hudson River Club
Island
J. G. Melon's
Jezebel

Jim McMullen
Joe Allen
Joe's Bar & Grill
K Paul's
Lox Around The
　Clock
Luke's Bar & Grill
Malabar
March
Memphis
Mesa Grill
Michael's
Mickey Mantle's
Mortimer's
Nathan's Famous
P.J. Clarke's
Polo Grounds
Prix Fixe
Ravelled Sleeve
River Café
Rose Café
Rusty Staub's on
　Fifth
Sam's Café
Sam's Restaurant
Saranac
Shelby's
Savoy
Sylvia's
Table d'Hôte
Three Guys, The
Time Café
Tony Roma's
TriBeCa Grill
Vince & Eddie's

BELGIAN
Café de Bruxelles

BRAZILIAN
Brazil 2000
Cabana Carioca
Coffee Shop

CARIBBEAN
Tropica

CHINESE
Au Mandarin
Auntie Yuan
Chez Vong
Chin Chin
China Grill
David K's
Fu's
H.S.F
Hunan Village
Kwong and Wong
Noodle Town
Our Place
Pig Heven
Shun Lee Palace
Silver Palace
Simon's
Siu Lam Kung
Sung Chiu Mei
Tse Yang
Wong Kee
Zen Palate

CONTINENTAL
"21" Club
Algonquin, The
Brandywine
Box Tree, The
Box Tree Kitchens
Café 44
Café des Artistes
Café Nicholson
Cellar in The Sky
Capsouto Frères
Delia's
Edwardian Room
540 Park
Ernie's
Four Seasons, The
Jockey Club, The

Keen's
Oak Room and Bar
Polo, The
Petrossian
Rainbow Room
Sardi's
Sign of The Dove
Tavern on The
Green
Terrace, The
Terry Dinan's
Union Square Café
Windows on the
World
World Yacht
Cruises

CUBAN
Bayamo
Sabor
Victor's Café 44

DELICATESSEN
Carnegie Deli
Katz's

ECLECTIC
Alison on Dominick
Ambassador Grill
B. Smith's
Camelback &
Central
Café Lucas
Café Society
Duane Park Café
Extra! Extra!
Gibbon, The
Gotham Bar & Grill
Jerry's
Koo Koo's Bistro
Mimosa
Metropolis
Mezzanine, The
Michael's
Mondrian
Montrachet
Onda

Post House
Quilted Giraffe
Saturnia
Soho Kitchen and
Bar
Sonia Rose
South Street
Seaport
Tatou
Zig Zag Bar & Grill

ETHIOPIAN
Abyssinia

FRENCH
Adrienne
Au Manoir
Au Troquet
Auberge Maxime
Bertrand
Bienvenue
Bistro Bamboche
Bistro Du Nord
Brasserie
Buffet de la Gare
Café
Café du Parc
Café Luxembourg
Café Metairie
Café Pierre
Café Loup
Chanterelle
Chez Pierre
Chez Josephine
Collage
Ferrier
Florent
Hulot's
Jean Lafitte
JoJo
Jour et Nuit
L'Acajou
L'Aubiniere
Lespinasse
L'Omnibus
L'Oustalet

La Boheme
La Caravelle
La Cité
La Colombe D'Or
La Côte Basque
La Gauloise
La Goulue
La Grange at the
Homestead Inn
La Grenouille
La Mangeoire
La Metairie
La Panetiere
La Petite Auberge
La Petite Ferme
La Reserve
La Table des Rois
Le Bilbouquet
Le Chantilly
Le Cirque
Le Comptoir
Le Pactole
Le Perigord
Le Pistou
Le Refuge
Le Regence
Le Relais
Le Train Bleu
Le Veau D'Or
Les Halles
Les Pleiades
Les Routiers
Lutèce
Madame Romaine
de Lyons
Mark's
Maurice
Maxim's
Maxime's
Nicole's
Odeon, The
Park Bistro
Poiret
Provence

Quatorze
Quatorze Bis
Raoul's
Restaurant Jean
  Louis
Restaurant
  Lafayette
Restaurant
  Raphael
Sel & Poivre
Un Deux Trois
Voulez Vous

GREEK
Periyali
Greek Village

HUNGARIAN
Mocca Restaurant

ICE CREAM
Rumpelmayer's
Serendipity

ITALIAN
Al Bacio
Albero D'Oro
Alfredo's the
  Original of Rome
Alo Alo
Amerigo's
Amici Miei
Ancora Pronto
Andiamo
Angelo's
Antico Caffe
Aria
Arqua
Azzurro
Barbetta
Barocco
Barolo
Bellini by Cipriani
Benito's II
Bice
Brio
Caffe Equesne

Café Sirocusa
Campagnola
Canastel
Ca'Nova
Capriccio
Carmine's
Cent'Anni
Cesarina
Chelsea Trattoria
Ciaobella
Coco Pazzo
Colors
Contrapunto
Corrado
Col Legno
Da Fiore
Da Noi
Da Silvano
Da Tommaso
Da Umberto
Divino
Dolce
Dominick's
Due
Ecco
Elaine's
Elio's
Ennio & Michael
Erminia
Felidia
Ferrara
Giambelli 50th
Gino
Girasole
Harry Cipriani
Il Cantinori
Il Cortile
Il Menestrello
Il Monello
Il Mulino
Il Nido
Il Valetto
Lattanzi
John's of Bleecker

Le Madri
Lello
Letizia
Lusardi's
Malvasia
Mamma Leone's
Manganaro
Marcello
Mario's
Mazzei
Mezzaluna
Mezzogiorno
Milanese
Nanni's
Natalino
Nicola Paone
Nicola's
Olio
Orso
Palio
Paola's
Paper Moon
Parioli
  Romanissimo
Patsy's
Petaluma
Pinnochio
Ponte's
Positano
Primavera
Primola
Remi
Romeo Salta
Rosolio
Saint Ambroeus
San Domenico
San Giusto
Sandro's
Scarlatti
Sette Mezzo
Sfuzzi
Sistina
Stella del Mare
Tempo

Tira Misu
Trastevere
Trattoria
Trattoria Dell'Arte
Tre Scalini
Triangulo
Trionfo
Via Via
Vico
Vico Madison
Villa Mosconi
Vivolo
Vucciria
Yellowfingers

IRISH
Reidy's

INDIAN
Akbar
Bombay Palace
Bukhara
Dawat
Jewel of India
Raga

JAPANESE
Hatsuhana
Mitsukoshi
Nippon
Omen
Seryna
Shinwa
Take-Zushi
Tatany

KOREAN
Woo Lae Oak of
  Seoul

MEDITERRANEAN
Café Crocodile
Eze

MEXICAN
Café Iguana
Caramba!!
El Parador
El Teddy's
José Sent Me
Rio Grande
Rosa Mexicano
Santa Fe
Zarela
Zona Rosa

**MIDDLE
EASTERN**
Al Amir
Al Bustan
The Nile

RUSSIAN
Russian Tea Room

SCANDINAVIAN
Aquavit

SEAFOOD
Dock's
Gloucester House
Grand Central
  Oyster Bar
John Clancy's East
John Clancy's
Manhattan Ocean
  Club
Pisces
Sea Grill
Sidewalkers
Sloppie Louie's
Water Club, The
Wilkinson's
  Seafood Café

SPANISH
Alcala
Café San Martin
Eldorado Petit
Malaga
Meson Botin
Paradis Barcelona
Sevilla
Solera

STEAK
Bruno's Pen &
  Pencil
Christ Cella
Gage & Tollner
Gallagher's
Market Dining
  Room
Peter Luger
Palm
Smith & Wollensky
Sparks Steak
  House

SWISS
Chalet Suisse

THAI
Bangkok Cuisine
Java
Puket
Tommy Tang

TURKISH
Anatolia
Istanbul Cuisine

VENEZUELAN
Mambo Grill

VIETNAMESE
Can
Indochine
Le Bar Bat

WHERE TO FIND THE BEST...

Apple Tart: Lutèce, Gotham Bar & Grill, Quatorze, River Café
BBQ: Carolina, Pig Heaven, Sylvia's, Mesa Grill
Bloody Mary: Melon's, P.J. Clarke's
Caesar Salad: Mark's, Milanese, Post House
Calf's Liver: Felidia, Le Madri, Vince & Eddie's
Carpaccio: Harry Cipriani (beef)
         Le Bernardin and Four Seasons (fish)
Caviar: Petrossian, Russian Tea Room
Cheesecake: Ca'Nova, Spark's, Mazzei
Cheese Cart: Parioli Romanissimo, Chanterelle, Le Pactole
Chili: Empire Diner, Mambo Grill
Chocolate Cake: An American Place, Four Seasons, Zarela's
Choucroute Garni: La Cité, Quatorze, Veau d'Or
Crab Cakes: Coach House, Gage & Tollner, Gloucester House
Crème Brûlée: Le Cirque, La Metairie, Mimosa
Espresso: Ferrara, Sandro's, Sistina
Foie Gras: Le Cirque, Montrachet, La Caravelle
French Fries: Quatorze Bis, Jerry's, Post House
Game: The Four Seasons, Michael's, Restaurant Jean-Louis
Guacamole: Rosa Mexicano, Zona Rosa, Santa Fe
Hamburger: "21" Club, J. G. Melon's, Post House
Hot Dogs: Katz's, Nathan's Famous, Serendipity
Ice Cream: Sandro's, Serendipity, Siracusa
Lobster: Manhattan Ocean Club, The Palm, Smith & Wollensky
Lobster (gourmet): Arcadia, Montrachet, San Domenico
Margaritas: Arizona 206, El Teddy's, El Parador
Oysters: Dock's, Manhattan Ocean Club,
         The Grand Central Oyster Bar
Pasta: Felidia, Il Nido, Parioli Romanissimo, Remi
Peking Duck: Auntie Yuan, China Grill, Shun Lee
Pizza: John's of Bleecker, Le Madri, Via Via, Col Legno
Profiteroles: Gotham Bar & Grill, Mortimer's, Collage
Rack of Lamb: Le Perigord, Parioli Romanissimo, Prix Fixe
Ribs: Sylvia's, Tony Roma's, Carolina
Risotto: Il Monello, Palio, San Domenico, Barbetta
Roast Chicken: La Caravelle, Lutèce, Union Square Café,
Salmon: Manhattan Ocean Club, Mimosa, La Caravelle
Sandwiches: Empire Diner, Carnegie Deli, Katz's
Smoked Salmon/Gravlax: Aquavit, Lutèce, Aureole
Soft-shell Crabs: Capsouto Frères, Sea Grill, Shun Lee

Soufflés: La Côte Basque, La Goulue, La Caravelle
Steak: The Palm, Smith & Wollensky, Spark's Steak House
Sushi: Hatsuhana, Mitsukoshi, Nippon, Shinwa
Sweetbreads: Café Pierre, The Quilted Giraffe, Bouley
Tandoor: Bukhara, Dawat, Raga
Tiramisu: San Domenico, Natalino, Vico, Mazzei
Veal Chop: Amerigo's, Scarlatti, Sette Mezzo, Ponte's
Vegetarian Dish: Lusardi's, Mambo Grill

WHERE SHOULD I GO FOR...

After Theater: Barbetta, Chez Josephine, Carolina
Anniversary/Birthday: Le Cirque, Lutèce, Parioli Romanissimo
Artsy: Delia, Odeon, Florent
Bar Scene: "21" Club, Mortimer's, P.J. Clarke's, Le Comptoir
Best Bargains: Le Pistou, Da Fiore, Natalino, Montrachet
Best New Arrivals: JoJo, Mimosa, L'Espinasse, Mesa Grill,
                Al Bustan
Bistro: Park Bistro, JoJo, Café, Ferrier, Café Loup
Brunch: Café des Artistes, Capsouto Frères, Gotham Bar & Grill
Business Meal (celebratory): Aureole, Bouley, Le Regence
Business Meal (serious): Four Seasons Grill Room,
                Lespinasse, Mondrian
Cabaret Music: Tatou, Mambo Grill (Wednesdays)
Celebrities: La Grenouille, Le Cirque, Russian Tea Room
Celebration: La Caravelle, Union Square Café,
                Gotham Bar & Grill
Children's Party: Mickey Mantle's, Malabar's, Serendipity
Christmas: American Festival Cafe, Tavern on The Green,
                Windows on the World
Dancing: Maxim's, The Rainbow Room (traditional) ,
                Tatou (trendy)
Dinner for One: Mark's, Madame Romaine de Lyons, Oyster Bar
Easter: Café Pierre, Edwardian Room, Tavern on The Green
Father's Day: The Coach House, The Oak Room, Water Club
Fireplaces: "21" Club, The Box Tree, Raphael
Floral Decorations: Aureole, Chanterelle, La Grenouille
Gardens: Barbetta, Provence, Restaurant Raphael, Barolo
Gourmet Foreigners: An American Place, Aureole,
                Gotham Bar & Grill
History: Fraunces Tavern, Gage & Tollner,
                Harvey's Chelsea Restaurant

Home Delivery: Bukhara, Dawat, Fu's
Hotel Restaurant: Edwardian Room (The Plaza),
                 Le Regence (Plaza Athenée),
                 Mark's (The Mark),
                 Ambassador Grill (UN Plaza)
Interior Design (modern): Eldorado Petit, Palio, Cafe 44
Interior Design (traditional): "21", Four Seasons, Rainbow Room
Ladies Who Lunch: La Grenouille, Le Cirque, Mortimer's
Late Night: Coffee Shop, Café Luxembourg, Florent, Jour et Nuit
"Lite" Cuisine: Café Pierre, The Four Seasons, Saturnia
Mother's Day: Sign of The Dove, Lespinasse, Edwardian Room
NYC Experience: "21" Club, P.J. Clarke's, The Palm
Out-of-Towners: Rainbow Room, River Café,
                 Windows on the World, World Yacht Cruises
Power Breakfast: 540 Park, Edwardian Room, "21" Club
Pre-Theater: La Caravelle, La Reserve, Orso
Private Dining Room (business): Mondrian, Rainbow Room
Private Dining Room (social): Le Cirque, La Grenouille,
                 Sign of The Dove, Remi
Romantic Dinner for Two: Café des Artistes, Le Perigord,
                 Restaurant Raphael, Ca'Nova
Service: Four Seasons, La Caravelle, Lutèce
Singles Scene: Café Lucas, Alo Alo, Jour et Nuit
Sports Scene: Mickey Mantle's, Polo Grounds, Rusty's on Fifth
Sunday: Cent'Anni, The Coach House, Mesa Grill
Tabletop Design: An American Place, John Clancy's East,
                 Quilted Giraffe
Teenager's Party: Cafe Iguana, Empire Diner, Hard Rock
                 Cafe, Le Bar Bat
Trendy: JoJo, Coco Pazzo, TriBeCa Grill
Views: The Rainbow Room, The River Café, The Terrace,
       Windows on the World, Hudson River Club, Le Pactole
Tea: Café Pierre, Saint Ambroeus, The Plaza
Worst Waits: Bouley, Coco Pazzo, Le Comptoir, JoJo

GOOD VALUE

(Where the bill should run between $25 to $30 per person)

Abyssinia
Acme Bar & Grill
Al Amir
Al Bustan
Albuquerque Eats
Alo Alo
America
Anatolia
Angelo's
Arizona Café
Azzurro
Bankok Cuisine
Benito's II
Bistro Bamboche
Bienvenue
Brio
Cabana Carioca
Café Crocodile
Café du Parc
Café Iguana
Café Loup
Carmine's
Cent'Anni
Chefs Cuisiniers Club
Coffee Shop
Col Legno
Collage
Da Fiore
Due
El Parador
Ferrier
Greek Village
Hunan Village
Istanbul Cuisine
J.G. Melon's
Jerry's
Katz's Delicatessen
Koo Koo's Bistro

Kwong & Wong
L'Acajou
La Boheme
Le Veau D'Or
Lox Around the Clock
Manganaro
Mario's
Mambo Grill
Metropolis
Mickey Mantle's
Mimosa
Mocca Restaurant
Montrachet
Natalino
Noodle Town
Onda
P.J. Clarke's
Pig Heavan
Prix Fixe
Provence
Quatorze
Sam's Café
Sarabeth's Kitchen
Saranac
Serendipity
Sevilla
Siracusa Gourmet Café
Siu Lam Kung
Soho Kitchen and Bar
Take-Sushi
Tatany
Triangulo
Tropica
Vasata
Via Via
Villa Mosconi
Vince & Eddie's
Wong Kee

Three to Five Star Ratings

★★★★★

Amerigo's
Aureole
Coach House, The
Felidia
Four Seasons, The
Gotham Bar and Grill
La Caravelle
Le Bernardin
Le Cirque
Le Perigord
Lutèce
Maxime's
Montrachet
San Domenico

★★★★ ½

An American Place
Il Nido
La Panetiere
Parioli Romanissimo
Restaurant Jean-Louis
Union Square Café

★★★★

"21" Club
Alison on Dominick
Ambassador Grill
Arcadia
Auberge Maxime
Barbetta
Bouley
Café Crocodile
Grand Central Oyster Bar
Hatsuhana
Il Monello
JoJo
La Reserve
Le Regence
Manhattan Ocean Club
Mark's Restaurant
Mazzei
Mondrian
Park Bistro

Quilted Giraffe, The
Remi
Scarlatti
Shun Lee
Shun Lee Palace
Sign of the Dove
Smith & Wollensky
Sparks Steak House
Terrace, The

★★★ ½

Aquavit
Bertrand
Buffet de la Gare
Ca'Nova
Café des Artistes
Café Pierre
Chanterelle
Dawat
Edwardian Room, The
Fu's
Harry Cipriani
Hunan Village
La Colombe D'Or
La Côte Basque
La Grenouille
La Metairie
Le Madri
Le Pistou
Lespinasse
Michael's
Nippon
Orso
Palm
Pig Heaven
Post House
Prix Fixe
Provence
Quatorze
Quatorze Bis
Rainbow Room, The
Sandro's
Sistina
Solera
Tribeca Grill

Vico Ristorante
Zarela
Zen Palate

Adrienne
Al Amir
Al Bustan
Alfredo's the Original
   of Rome
Alo Alo
Anatolia
Aria
Arizona 206
Arqua
Au Troquet
Azzurro
Bellini by Cipriani
Bistro du Nord
Bombay Palace
Box Tree, The
Bruno's Pen & Pencil
Bukhara
Café
Café Du Parc
Café Luxembourg
Can
Capsouto Frères
Carolina
Cellar in the Sky
Cent'Anni
Chelsea Trattoria
Chin Chin
Coco Pazzo
Da Silvano
Elio's
Empire Diner, The
Ennio & Michael
Ferrier
Gino
Gloucester House
Hulot's
Il Valletto
Il Menetsrello
La Cité
La Crèmaillére
La Grange at the
   Homestead Inn

La Petite Ferme
Le Bilboquet
Le Pactole
Le Refuge
Le Train Bleu
Le Veau D'Or
Lello
Les Pleiades
Lusardi's
Madame Romaine de Lyons
Malvasia
Mambo Grill
Mario's
Market Dining Rooms, The
Maxim's
Mesa Grill
Mezzaluna
Milanese
Mimosa
Mitsukoshi
Mortimer's
Natalino
Oak Room and Bar, The
Palio
Paola's Restaurant
Petrossian
Pinocchio
Pinocchio Ristorante
Primola
Restaurant Lafayette
Restaurant Raphael
Rosa Mexicano
Saturnia
Sette Mezzo
Sevilla
Simon's
Siracusa Gourmet Café
Siu Lam Kung
Table d'Hôte
Tavern on the Green
Tempo
Tommy Tang
Triangolo
Via Via
Vico Madison
Vince & Eddie's

OPEN LATE

Alo Alo
Amsterdam's Bar
  & Rotisserie
B. Smith's
Barolo
Bayamo
Bistro du Nord
Brazil 2000
Café
Campagnola
Canastel
Capsouto Frères
Carmine's
Century Café, The
Chez Josephine
Coco Pazzo
Contrapunto
Corrado
Elio's
Ernie's
Felidia
Ferrara

Ferrier
Gallagher's
H.S.F.
Harvey's Chelsea
  Restaurant
Island
La Cité
Le Comptoir
Les Halles
Lusardi's
Mambo Grill
Metropolis
Mr. Chow
Nicola's
Petaluma
Petrossian
Poiret
Polo Grounds
Primavera
Primola
Prix Fixe
Quatorze

Quatorze Bis
Rainbow Room,
  The
Rosa Mexicano
Rumpelmayer's
Russian Tea Room
San Domenico
Santa Fe
Saranac
Sfuzzi
Shun Lee
Soho Kitchen
  and Bar
Tatou
Time Café
TriBeCa Grill
Un Deux Trois
Via Via
Vico
Vince & Eddie's

OPEN AFTER MIDNIGHT

Acme Bar & Grill
Brasserie
  (24 hours)
Café des Artistes
Café Luxembourg
Chefs Cuisiniers
  Club
Ciaobella
Coconut Grill
Contrapunto
Delia's
Elaine's
Empire Diner
  (24 hours)

Florent (24 hours)
Hard Rock Café
Indochine
J. G. Melon's
Java
Jezebel
Jim McMullen
Joe Allen
Joe's Bar & Grill
Jour et Nuit
La Cité (Grill)
Le Bar Bat
Le Madri

Lox Around The
  Clock (24 hrs
  on weekends)
Mezzaluna
Nile, The
Odeon, The
P.J. Clarke's
Reidy's
River Café, The
Yellowfingers
Zig Zag Bar
  & Grill

SUNDAY SUGGESTIONS

B = Brunch only **D = Dinner only** **B&D = Brunch & Dinner**

Al Amir ....B&D
Al Bustan......B&D
American Festival
  Café.............B&D
Amerigo's .....B&D
Auberge
  Maxime......B&D
Bellini ....D
Bice.....................D
Box Tree, TheB&D
Café................B&D
Café des
  Artistes .....B&D
Café
  Luxembourg..B&D
Café Pierre.....B&D
Can ....B&D
Capsouto
  Frères ....B&D
Carmine's .....B&D
Cent'Anni...........D
China Grill ....D
Chin Chin ....D
Coach House, The.D
Coco Pazzo ....B&D
Dawat ....D
Da Silvano .....B&D
Da Tommaso .B&D
Edwardian
  Room ....B&D
Elio's...................D
Empire Diner.B&D
El Parador .....B&D
Ferrier ....B&D
Florent...........B&D
Gage &
  Tollner ....B&D

Gino ....B&D
Gotham Bar
  & Grill ....D
Harry
  Cipriani.......B&D
Il Cantinori ....D
Java ....D
Jerry's..................B
Lespinasse .....B&D
L'Oustalet ....D
La Cité ....D
La Gauloise ....B
La Metairie ....B&D
La Panetiere ..B&D
Le Comptoir.......D
Le Madri ....D
Le Pactole ....B
Le Regence ....B&D
Les Halles ......B&D
Lusardi's.............D
Madame Romaine
  de Lyons ....B
Mambo Grill ..B&D
Manhattan Ocean
  Club ....D
Mario's ....B&D
Mark's ....B&D
Maxime's ....B&D
Mazzei ....D
Mesa Grill ......B&D
Michael's ....B&D
Mimosa..........B&D
Mortimer's.........D
Nicola's ....D
Odeon, The ....B
Omen ....D
Park Bistro ....D

Poiret ....D
Primavera...........D
Primola ....D
Provence........B&D
Quatorze Bis ....D
Quatorze ....D
Rainbow Room ...D
Raoul's................D
Remi ....B&D
River Café,
  The ....B&D
Russian Tea
  Room, The .B&D
Sabor ....D
Saranac ....B&D
San Domenico ...D
Sea Grill........B&D
Sette Mezzo ....D
Shun Lee........B&D
Shun Lee
  Palace ....B&D
Sign of the
  Dove............B&D
Silver Palace..B&D
Sistina................D
Siu Lam KungB&D
Smith &
  Wollensky ...B&D
Table D'Hote .B&D
Tavern on
  The Green...B&D
Vico.....................D
Vince &
  Eddie's........B&D
Windows on
  the World.........B
Zen Palate .....B&D

144

WORTHY WINE LISTS

"21" Club
Aureole
An American Place
Bice
Cafe San Martin
Felidia
Four Seasons, The
Grand Central Oyster Bar
Il Monello
Il Nido
La Caravelle
La Cité
La Côte Basque
La Goulue
La Metairie
Le Bernardin
Le Cirque
Le Perigord
Lusardi's

Lutèce
Manhattan Ocean Club
Michael's
Mondrian
Montrachet
Palio
Post House, The
Quilted Giraffe, The
Rainbow Room, The
Restaurant Raphael
River Café, The
Rusty Staub's on Fifth
San Domenico
Sign of the Dove
Smith & Wollensky
Sparks Steak House
Union Square Café
Windows on the World

FOR CHILDREN

The following restaurants are suggested for families with children: We've found them to be particularly well suited because of the friendly atmosphere and staff attitude.

Albuquerque Eats
Alfredo's the Original of
   Rome
American Festival Café
Amerigo's
Azzurro
Bayamo
Carmine's
Empire Diner, The
Ennio & Michael

Extra! Extra!
Gargiulo's
Lox Around the Clock
Malabar
Mamma Leone's
Mickey Mantle's
Serendipity
Saranac
Tavern on the Green
Tony Roma's

TAKE-OUT

Acme Bar & Grill
Albero D'Oro
Albuquerque Eats
Alfredo's the Original
   of Rome
All American Diner
Amerigo's
Amsterdam's Bar & Grill
Au Mandarin
Bangkok Cuisine
Barocco
Bayamo
BBQ
Bistro du Nord
Bombay Palace
Brazil 2000
Bukhara
Cabana Carioca
Caramba
Carnegie Deli
Chin Chin
Coastal
Coconut Grill
Corrado
David K's
Dawat
Da Umberto
Extra! Extra!
Ferrara
Florent
Fu's
Grand Central Oyster Bar
Harvey's Chelsea
   Restaurant
Hatsuhana
H.S.F.
Java
J. G. Melon's
John's of Bleecker
Katz's

Les Halles
Lox Around the Clock
Malaga
Manganaro
Mario's
Mezzaluna
Mocca Restaurant
Mr. Chow
Nippon
Our Place
Palm, The
Pig Heaven
Post House
Puket
Quilted Giraffe
Raga
Ravelled Sleeve, The
Rio Grande
Romeo Salta
Russian Tea Room
Rusty Staub's on Fifth
Shinwa
Shun Lee Palace
Sidewalkers
Simon's
Siracusa
Siu Lam Kung
Soho Kitchen & Bar
Sung Chu Mei
Sylvia's
Take-Zushi
Tatany
Three Guys, The
Trattoria
Victor's Café 52
Via Via
Woo Lae Oak of Seoul
Zig Zag Bar & Grill
Zen Palate

PASSPORT
Vintage Wine Chart

Wine	'74	'75	'76	'77	'78	'79	'80	'81	'82	'83	'84	'85	'86	'87	'88	'89	'90
Beaujolais															9	9	9
Red Bordeaux	6	9	7	6	9	6	7	8B	8B	9B	5	9B	8A	6	9A	10A	9A
Red Burgundy			7	5	8	6	8	6	6	5	9B	5	9B	7B	9A	9A	10A
White Burgundy			8	5	9	6	8	7	6	8B	6	8	9	7	8B	10A	9A
Rhône			6	7	8	6	7	7	8	9B	5	9A	8B	6A	8A	9A	9A
Barolo			9	7	8	6	9	7	6	8B	8B	9A	7A	7B	8A	9A	9A
Chianti				9	5	6	6	8	6	7	5	10A	7A	7B	8A	9A	9A
Cabernet			9	7	7	7	8	7	7	9	5	9B	7B	7A	8A	9A	9A
Chardonnay					8	8	8	8	7	7	6	7	8	9	8	8B	9A

Select Vintages

Sauternes	'89A '88A '86A '85A '83A '76 '75 '71 '67
German White	'89A '88A '85A '82B '79 '76 '71
Champagne	'85A '83 '82 '79 '76 '73
Classic Claret	'70 '66 '61 '59 '55 '53 '49 '47 '45
Vintage Port	'55 '60 '63 '66 '70 '75B '77B '80B '83A '85A

A = needs more Aging
B = drinkable now, but could Benefit from more aging